COMPLAINING FOR JUSTICE
knowing your rights as a consumer
and how to get even not mad

COMPLAINING FOR JUSTICE

knowing your rights as a consumer
and how to get even not mad

Duncan Callow
LL.B Barrister

Otter Publications
Chichester, England

First published in 1998 by **OTTER PUBLICATIONS**, 9 Roman Way, Fishbourne, Chichester, West Sussex, PO19 3QN.

DISCLAIMER
Whilst the information herein is supplied in good faith, no responsibility is taken by either the publisher or the author for any damage, injury or loss, however caused, which may arise from the use of the information provided.

British Library Cataloging in Publication Data
A CIP record for this book is available from the British Library.
ISBN 1 899053 11 5

Acknowledgements
My thanks to Elaine Austin yet again for her faultless typing. And to Maria for keeping me going.

Text design by Angela Hutchings.
Cover design by Jim Wilkie.
All cartoons by Simon Golding.
Printed and bound in Great Britain by MPG Books Limited, Bodmin, Cornwall.
Distributed in the UK by Grantham Book Services, Isaac Newton Way, Alma Park Industrial Estate, Grantham, Lincolnshire, NG31 9SD.
The Otter Publications logo is reproduced from original artwork by David Kitt.

Table of Contents

Introduction

Heaven forbid that we should ever become as litigious a nation as the United States. It seems that where there's an opportunity for a lawyer to make some cash, a claim will follow. But in this country, accessing justice is still a complex and potentially expensive exercise. With legal aid in disarray and other forms of funding litigation still in their infancy, the consumer stands to get a raw deal.

Customer service can take one of three forms. Firstly, the overwhelming American-style, "have a nice life" approach. Secondly, the very British, "yes Sir, no Sir" stand or finally the, "get lost, service is a dirty word" attitude. But as consumers we have the right to an effective and responsive after sales service. Car manufacturers operate vast Customer Assistance Centres to deal with a multitude of complaints. Whilst their effectiveness has been brought into question, at least there is a set procedure for the consumer to follow. Other suppliers of goods and services may be lagging behind somewhat. This can make effective complaining very difficult. Lost letters, unanswered telephone calls and apparent disinterest can very soon make for frosty relations. Complaining for Justice has been written to help. It's a simple guidebook which highlights the relevant law and how to use it to its greatest effect. Necessarily I haven't covered every consumer transaction. My knowledge and a requirement to keep the book as user-friendly as possible have meant that there are gaps. But much of the secret to effective complaining is common to all purchases.

It is not intended as a replacement for professional advice. I also don't wish to turn us into a nation of whingers. My philosophy is simple - know the relevant law, complain early and effectively and be prepared to compromise. Fighting solely on a point of principle might make you feel better but it's unlikely to bear fruit. It'll also clog up the system for genuine complainers.

Enjoy the book.

Duncan Callow
Surrey

Chapter 1

A Shopper's Paradise?

There can be no escaping the fact that we are a nation of shoppers. Stores are bigger, brighter, better designed and open at times to suit the customer. Some have crèches and other facilities to entertain the children whilst you shop to your heart's (but not your wallet's) content. At the bigger out of town complexes, access and parking are easy and when you've done the week's grocery shopping you can call in for a pizza or catch a matinee at the on-site multiplex cinema. Surely a paradise for shoppers? Possibly - even probably if you have the money to spend. But don't think for a minute that the retailers exist for your convenience - they want as much of your cash as they can possibly get their hands on. And if it's not actually your cash, then they'll just as happily take your plastic. A no-lose situation for the retailers but what about you the consumer? What if, through clever marketing, you've been tempted to buy something that you don't really want? Is there such a thing as a cooling-off period to allow you to change your mind? What are your rights if the goods are in some way lacking or dangerous? How do you act effectively to get your money back? What if you've paid by credit card - is the situation any different? What if you have no receipt or the goods were bought as a present for someone else who simply doesn't like them? What if you've bought items in a sale - are your rights diluted in any way?

All of these questions and many more besides, are asked every day. The more we shop, the greater the scope for complaint. Knowing your rights on the High Street (or more probably out of town retail park!) is essential to the 1990's shopper. More important still, is knowing how to enforce those rights.

There is much confusion amongst shoppers as the lines between law and customer policy become ever more blurred. If one of the major retailers offers a no-quibbles refunds policy whatever the "problem" but the next one offers no more protection than it is obliged to do by law, it becomes clear why consumers are confused about their rights.

1.1 PAYING FOR THE GOODS
Legal tender
For many people, cash is still the chosen method of payment. But there may be one or two surprises. Legal tender is the amount which a retailer is obliged to take in payment for the goods. Bank of England notes and gold coins are legal for the payment of any amount. But 5p and 10p pieces are only legal tender for payments of up to £5. For 20p and 50p pieces this figure rises to £10 but a retailer only has to accept your coppers up to a value of 20p! Curiously it is also worth noting that a retailer is not legally obliged to give change, the exact sum must be tendered.

Scottish/Northern Irish bank notes
These are not legal in England and Wales. However, some retailers may accept them.

Credit cards
These are an increasingly popular way to pay for goods and services because they are convenient (no need to carry cash) and you can "buy now, worry later". They are also very useful because under S.75 of the Consumer Credit Act 1974 you have a claim against the card issuer in the event that you get into a dispute with the retailer (merchant) which you cannot resolve. This protection applies as long as the price of the individual item purchased was over £100. It is the total price of the item which matters, not the amount of credit.

CASE HISTORY
Elaine bought a new crash helmet for her husband Barry who's a keen motorcyclist. It cost her £120 - £70 of which was paid in cash, the balance of £50 being charged to her credit card. After one week the visor had snapped off the helmet making it unsafe to use. She complained to the retailer concerned. It didn't want to know so she pursued the credit card company too. Because the total purchase price was over £100, S.75 applied so Elaine was able to secure a full refund.

⚖ TIPPING THE SCALES OF JUSTICE ⚖

The Consumer Credit Act offers valuable protection in cases of faulty goods and services. It can also help out where you've left a deposit on a card with a retailer which later goes out of business.

Some credit card companies also offer purchase protection insurance. For example, if you have no other relevant insurance and drop the valuable vase which you've just bought, you may be covered for a replacement.

Because credit cards are so popular and so widely accepted, they are very attractive to thieves. If you lose a card or think that it's been stolen, you won't be liable for any misuse of it after you've notified the company concerned. Up to the point of notification your financial liability is capped at *£50*.

Credit cards are used to pay for many different goods and services over the telephone - airline tickets, theatre tickets, car insurance etc. There is understandably a fear that once you've given out your number, anyone could be using your card to book their next Caribbean holiday. Fortunately such abuse is not nearly as widespread as you might imagine and in such cases your liability would be nil. Of more concern is the practice of signing blank credit card vouchers. Don't do this. Fill in all the boxes and be absolutely clear what you're agreeing to. Once you've given your signature, the credit card company will argue that you've given your blanket authorisation. The problem is most often encountered in foreign restaurants.

CASE HISTORY

Jim and Sarah went off to Barbados on their honeymoon. Still feeling ecstatic with his new wife, Jim signed a blank Visa card voucher in a rustic restaurant. Having probably drunk one beer too many, he agreed to let the restaurant manager "fill in the details". On his return to the UK, Jim was faced with a bill of over £200 which he had to pay.

When shopping around for a new credit card, be very careful not to get taken in by the glossiest literature. Whilst credit cards are valuable because you can pay back what you've borrowed over an indefinite period, there is a price to be paid. Interest. The longer you take to repay your balance and the greater the interest charged, the more money the card issuer makes. Check the small print very carefully - look for the Annual Percentage Rate (APR). This figure typically ranges from 14% right up to 30%. It is the APR which is the accurate measure of how much one credit card company charges for its credit compared with another.

If you are struggling to keep up with your repayments, contact the card issuer IMMEDIATELY. It may freeze the interest or offer a repayment "holiday" whereby no interest accrues for a few months. If you simply fail to keep up the repayments, the card issuer will blacklist you and eventually sue for the entire sum outstanding.

If your credit card account is being mishandled or there are phantom charges, always complain in writing to the card issuer. Your ultimate complaint lies with the Office of Fair Trading.

Debit and charge cards

These are quite different from credit cards. A debit card works in just the same way as a cheque. You sign a sales voucher and in two or three days, the amount is debited from you account. Such cards are not regulated by the Consumer Credit Act and they carry no charges or interest. Typical examples are Connect and Switch.

Charge cards, such as American Express and Diners Club, give you the worldwide flexibility of a credit card but with no interest charges. For an annual fee of around £40 the company gives you an unlimited amount of free credit for about one month. When the bill arrives you must pay it in full. A Gold Card works on the same principle but gives added benefits such as free insurance and travel incentives. It also costs about twice as much as a "standard" charge card.

In respect of debit cards, complain first to your branch manager, then to his regional manager and ultimately to the Banking Ombudsman.

Cheques

These are often referred to as cash and to all intents and purposes, have the same effect. However the retailer concerned does not have to accept a cheque, especially if the amount is more than that guaranteed by your card (£50, £100, £250). If your cheque book is stolen and you let the bank/building society know as soon as possible, then you won't be liable for any fraudulent use of those cheques. But if your cheque guarantee card is stolen at the same time, you *may* be liable. This is because one of the conditions of use is that the two are kept separate and apart.

If you write "Account Payee" on the face of a crossed cheque, you won't be liable if a stolen cheque is paid into a thief's account.

Many people stop a cheque after they've bought goods and services. This may be because they change their minds or there is a problem with the purchase. Technically, stopping a cheque is unlawful and the retailer deprived of your money can sue and obtain an immediate judgment.

⚖ TIPPING THE SCALES OF JUSTICE ⚖

In nearly all cases, stopping a cheque is dangerous. If there is a problem with your purchase, the law does not regard stopping payment as being a fair way to deal with it. Such a measure is sure to aggravate the retailer and you would be much less likely to reach an amicable solution.

Many retailers subscribe to various cheque guarantee schemes such as Transax. In much the same way as a credit card transaction is authorised, cheques are cleared for more than the value of the accompanying cheque guarantee card. But if you stop the cheque, the organisation concerned will then pursue you very hard (and without sympathy) for the sum in question. They effectively buy the debt from the retailer.

Invitations to treat

This is not a new way to get someone to buy you a bigger and better birthday present. But it is an important legal concept which confuses many consumers.

CASE HISTORY

Keith collects lampshades. One day he finally tracked down a particularly sought after and valuable shade to a shop in Brighton. It was on display in the window with a price of £75 clearly marked. Keith entered and asked the shopkeeper if he could look at the shade with a view to paying the full asking price. But the retailer told Keith that there had been a mistake and the shade was not for sale. Keith couldn't accept this and tried to rely on the law which protects consumers - he felt that because the item was clearly on display, with a price attached, the retailer had to sell it. In fact there is no law to protect in cases such as this. The fact that an item is in a shop window is an invitation to treat - an invitation to go to the retailer and make an offer to buy. But if the shop realises that it has made a mistake, it doesn't have to sell you the item. Keith had no case.

In fact retailers don't *have* to sell you anything on display in their shops. Even the price indicated is not the price which has to be accepted. But once you've made an offer which the retailer accepts, a contract is binding and enforceable, even if there is no written proof.

Illegal pricing

Invitations to treat are one thing, but a retailer can commit a criminal offence if he offers goods for sale at one price and then knowingly demands a higher price. The Trade Descriptions Act says that it is an offence to indicate that goods advertised for sale are being offered at a lower price than that at which they are in fact being offered.

If you are worried that a retailer is misleading its customers or applying false descriptions, contact your local council immediately and ask to speak to a Trading Standards Officer (TSO). The days of the price sticker gun are numbered. Although the Price Marking Order 1991 requires the price to be displayed on most goods, it is quite sufficient for a supermarket to show the price on the shelf. With technological advances it won't be long before each section of goods is displayed with an electronic digital read-out which can be varied even throughout the course of a trading day.

Deposits

Again a confusing area of the law. Deposits have two main functions. Firstly, a small deposit can be left against an item to "hold" it for you. Often deposits are made several weeks before Christmas on such a basis. Secondly, much larger deposits, perhaps as much as 50% of the purchase price are left because the retailer concerned has to make an investment of time and money to either the manufacturer or to source the item you want. In both cases however, you will have entered into a valid and binding contract. If you change you mind about the item or decide that you can't afford it, be prepared for the consequences. Not only will the retailer keep the deposit but it may try to recover its lost profit. This will be most likely where you have specified a particular design or size etc. and the retailer concerned has great difficulty in finding another purchaser.

⚖ TIPPING THE SCALES OF JUSTICE ⚖

If you must leave a deposit, make it small. Check carefully the conditions upon which it is left.

If, between leaving the deposit and taking delivery, the retailer concerned goes out of business, you can probably say goodbye to your deposit (unless the deposit was made by credit card, see previously).

1.2 ORDERING GOODS

Often the retailer either won't have the item you want in stock or will have to arrange for it to be delivered directly from the manufacturer. Usually furniture, soft furnishings, carpets (and of course new cars!) will be ordered well in advance of them being supplied. You'll probably be asked to sign an order form and leave a deposit. Once you do this, you are locked into a contract. Check the small print very carefully. If you change your mind or think that you can't afford the item, cancellation could be an expensive exercise. At the very least expect to lose your deposit. Really nasty retailers could even threaten to sue you for their loss of profit on the sale. Whether this threat turns into a reality will depend largely upon how quickly the goods you ordered can be resold. Retailers are under a duty to mitigate their losses but if what you've ordered is unusual or to a specific design etc., then you could be in for a fight!

The order form should clearly spell out the terms of the contract. In particular, look out for delivery dates, payment details and exclusion/limitation of liability clauses. The Unfair Terms in Consumer Contracts Regulations basically outlaw "unfair" terms. Of course this begs the definition of unfair;

> "*a contractual term which has not been individually negotiated is unfair if, contrary to the requirements of good faith, it causes a significant imbalance in the parties rights and obligations ..... to the detriment of the consumer*".

It is also worth remembering that the terms of the contract have to be made clear to you at the time of placing your order.

CASE HISTORY

Mr and Mrs Gopal ordered a new carpet from a local department store. They were given the store's standard trading conditions which they read, understood and agreed to. The carpet they'd ordered had actually gone out of production so the Gopals asked for all their money back. The store tried to rely on a little sign above the sales counter which read, *"In the event of carpet unavailability we reserve the right to supply a substitute. No refunds will be given"*.

The department store was taken to court and lost on two counts. Firstly, this term was not sufficiently well communicated at the time of the order and secondly, even if properly communicated, it would have been unfair.

⚖ TIPPING THE SCALES OF JUSTICE ⚖

When ordering goods and leaving a deposit, always try to use a credit card. If the company goes bust before delivery, you'll have a claim against the credit card company.

1.3 DELIVERY DELAYS

Goods must be delivered within a "reasonable period". Most goods are sold on the basis that the time for delivery is not of the essence of the contract. So if you're promised your new furniture within 6 - 8 weeks and it doesn't arrive on time, you can't cancel the contract. But if you are faced with delays:

- Write to the retailer.
- Make time of the essence.
- Give a deadline.
- If delivery is not within the deadline, confirm that you'll be in a position to treat the contract as over. You should then be refunded any sums paid.

1.4 WHAT CAN YOU EXPECT OF YOUR GOODS?

The governing law is the Sale and Supply of Goods Act 1994 (SSGA). As far as consumer sales are concerned, burn the following into your memory. Goods must:

1. **Belong to the person selling them** - if they belong to someone else, for example if they're stolen, you won't get to own them, even if you buy in good faith.

2. **Be of satisfactory quality** - what you'd expect of goods - their appearance, durability and freedom from minor defects should all be considered.
3. **Be fit for their purposes** - if you buy a waterproof coat which leaks water, it's not fit for its purpose.
4. **Match any sample you've been given** - for example if you buy carpet on the basis of a small sample, it should match that sample.

If the goods fail in one or more of these strict legal requirements you have a claim against the person who sold them - the retailer. Don't be fobbed off. You don't need to get involved with the manufacturer/supplier/wholesaler and any attempt to sidetrack you down such a route *must* be resisted. If the goods are faulty you can take them back and insist on a refund or replacement. Reasonable out of pocket expenses should also be added to you claim.

The difficulty with rejecting goods is that you can only do so if they've not been 'accepted'.

CASE HISTORY

John bought a colour TV in May 1996. By December of that year the tube needed replacing. He wanted his money back. He took the retailer to court using the small claims procedure. The District Judge found for the retailer. John had had the TV for too long - legally he'd 'accepted' it so his remedy was damages, i.e. the cost of repairing the TV.

If the TV had remained unused and in its box, then John would have been in a much stronger position to argue non-acceptance - even after 8 months. It's difficult to say what constitutes "acceptance" and every case will turn on its own facts. The SSGA is a relatively new piece of legislation and it does give consumers the right to have the faulty item repaired without losing the right of rejection. But it's not been properly tested through the courts, so for the time being the safest advice is to reject early.

∭ TIPPING THE SCALES OF JUSTICE ∭

- *Complain early, act quickly.*
- *Write it all down - keep notes.*
- *Have an idea of your legal rights - don't go in all guns blazing if you don't have a case.*
- *Target your complaint at someone in a position to do something about it.*
- *Be reasonable.*
- *Stay calm.*

- *Consider a compromise.*
- *Don't let emotions and principles get in the way of hard facts - you'll lose.*

1.5 PROOF OF PURCHASE
To reject or replace goods you'll have to prove that you bought them. Proof of purchase includes a receipt, a credit card voucher, a photocopy of a cheque, a witness or even a garment tag with the company name on it. Without this proof, the retailer is not obliged to offer any kind of recompense (although in practice, many do).

1.6 IT'S THE WRONG COLOUR
If you buy or have bought for you something which is unsuitable, perhaps the wrong size or colour, then you have no *right* to insist on a replacement or refund. The law simply says hard cheese to you. But of course many retailers realise the importance of keeping their customers sweet and operate an exchange/refunds policy. This is purely in addition to your legal rights and part of the reason why consumers are so confused. If one retailer operates such a policy surely it must be the law? If there is nothing wrong with the goods you may be offered nothing, a full refund, an exchange or a credit note entitling you to buy something else at a later date. Credit notes are *not* acceptable when goods are in any way defective. If a retailer tries to fob you off with one, contact your local TSO.

1.7 GOODS BOUGHT ON SALE
If you buy goods in the sales at knock-down prices, you still have exactly the same rights as if you paid the full pre-sale price. Some retailers try to avoid your rights by putting up notices such as, "No refunds on sale goods" or, "Sale goods cannot be returned".

These are illegal. A retailer which offers a refunds/exchange policy for non-faulty goods may withdraw it during the sales. This is OK but any attempt to get around your rights in respect of faulty goods is not. If the retailer is making a comparison of prices in the sale the law says that;

- The previous price should be the last price at which the goods were available in the previous six months.
- The goods should have been available at the higher price for at least 28 consecutive days during the previous six months.
- The goods should have been on sale at that higher price in the same shop (not another branch in another part of the country).

1.8 BUYING AT AUCTION

Many people buy cars and furniture at auction. There are undoubtedly bargains to be had. The risk however is that the auctioneer will contract out of his legal obligations to sell satisfactory quality and fit for their purpose goods. Check the auction particulars very carefully. If the SSGA has been excluded then you buy as a non-consumer and effectively have no rights. Also, once the hammer comes down for the last time, the bidding is over and you will be locked into a contract which you can't back out of. Usually you'll have to pay by cash or with a banker's draft and remove the goods from the auction house within 24 hours. If in doubt, take an experienced bidder with you and check the goods carefully before you get carried away.

1.9 BUYING PRIVATELY/AT A JUMBLE SALE/ AT A CAR BOOT SALE

If you buy privately then the only bit of the SSGA which applies is that the goods sold must match their description.

CASE HISTORY

Janet wanted a new washing machine. She looked through the small adds of her local paper and eventually found the ideal machine;

"6 month old Zanussi Washer Drier. Perfect order, only £150"

She went to view the machine and subsequently paid the £150. The private seller again confirmed that it was only 6 months old and had barely been used. Within a week the motor had burned out. The engineer called out by Janet told her that the machine was at least three years old and had seen very heavy use. On this basis she was entitled to claim the cost of repair from the seller.

The position is the same when buying from a car boot sale. In most cases you'll be pretty much unprotected - but that's half the fun of looking for the real bargains.

The situation is changing. Many people now trade commercially at car boot sales. If you can prove this, then full SSGA protection applies. Look out for familiar faces selling boxes of counterfeit goods. Many defective and in some cases dangerous electrical items are also sold through car boot sales. If you suspect that a dealer is responsible, take as many details as you can - ideally a name and address or vehicle details and report your findings to the local TSO.

1.10 STOLEN GOODS

The basic rule is that a seller cannot pass on a better title than he himself possesses. So if you buy goods which turn out to be stolen, even if in good faith, you never actually own them. They are still the lawful possessions of the person from whom they were stolen. If you find yourself in such a situation, the police will probably seize the goods pending court action. Your remedy would be to sue the seller for the full purchase price. Buying stolen goods is seldom a problem from a retailer. It is often bad news however when buying privately. If you're in any doubt at all, don't buy.

⚖ TIPPING THE SCALES OF JUSTICE ⚖

- *Always buy from the seller's home - never in a pub car park.*
- *Check any papers carefully - always ask to see invoices, service receipts etc.*
- *Does the seller know much about what he's selling? - if he's a bit vague, the chances are he's not had it for very long.*

1.11 MAIL ORDER

Again this is becoming an increasingly popular way to shop and in most cases it's perfectly safe. Indeed if you respond to a catalogue or magazine advertisement etc., you're probably even better protected. The SSGA applies in just the same way as if you're shopping on the High Street. There are several mail order protection schemes. The Mail Order Traders' Association for example states that you must be given at least 14 days to return unwanted goods. You don't have this right when buying elsewhere. If you run into problems, these schemes usually operate an arbitration procedure.

Always look to see if the retailer belongs to a scheme. Many small-ad advertisers are much less reputable so you do take a bit of a risk. To minimise this, check to see that the advertisement reappears on a regular basis. Make a few phone calls to see what kind of an outfit you're dealing with. You could even contact your local TSO to see if any complaints have been made. Never send cash. Ideally pay by credit card for extra protection. Check the small print - some advertisers may ask you to pay for return package and postage. How long is the anticipated wait time? If it's any more than 28 days, find out why. Make sure everything is well documented - if you have to go to court, you'll need good evidence.

1.12 EXPERTS

In most cases, responsible retailers will accept faulty goods without question. In some cases however you will need an expert opinion.

CASE HISTORY

Janice bought a new three piece suite. She paid over £3,500. After six months the material on one of the armchairs had started to wear very badly. Janice argued with the retailer that it wasn't of satisfactory quality. The retailer argued that it was due to fair wear and tear. A deadlock was reached. Janice then contacted an upholstery expert. His written report confirmed that the material was substandard and that the armchair should be replaced. Once the retailer saw the report it cooperated fully by giving Janice a new chair and by refunding the cost of the expert's report.

1.13 DANGEROUS GOODS

If you buy goods which are in some way dangerous or defective and result in damage to property or in personal injury, you have a direct claim against the manufacturer even if you didn't actually buy the item.

⚖ TIPPING THE SCALES OF JUSTICE ⚖

The Consumer Protection Act 1987 creates a form of strict liability on the part of suppliers/manufacturers. This means that if damage or personal injury totalling more than £275 is the result of defective goods, you don't have to prove any negligence. You only have to prove a defect - the product is less safe than a consumer is reasonably entitled to expect.

CASE HISTORY

Mr and Mrs Crapnell bought a new freezer for their daughter. Whilst she was away from her home, a motor in the freezer burned out resulting in a small fire. Around £800 of damage was caused. Because a defect in the motor was clearly proven, the daughter was able to pursue the manufacturer successfully. This was possible even though *she* hadn't bought the freezer.

1.14 GUARANTEES/WARRANTIES

Remember that when you buy goods your contract is with the retailer. It is responsible to make good if you encounter problems. However, many manufacturers also offer additional protection in the form of a guarantee - typically for 12 months. To activate the guarantee you'll usually have to send a card back to the manufacturer with proof of where and when the item was purchased.

In practice, most consumers don't rely on the guarantee. After all, this protection is purely in addition to your rights under the SSGA and something of a sales gimmick.

1.15 ENFORCING YOUR RIGHTS

So you've complained effectively, you've got evidence of all your losses and an expert's report to boot. But still the retailer isn't interested. Which way do you turn? You've essentially two options.

1. If the retailer/supplier is a member of a trade association, you could invoke its arbitration/complaints procedure. See the Databank section for full details.
2. Sue using the small claims procedure of the county court. Over 1.5 million small claims (currently the limit is for claims of up to £3,000) were started in 1995. The procedure must therefore provide a satisfactory remedy for many aggrieved consumers.

⚖ *TIPPING THE SCALES OF JUSTICE* ⚖

The small claims court is a relatively quick, cheap and easy to use remedy. But only fight if you have both a well supported case and the time to prepare properly.

Chapter 1 - Databank

Mediation UK
82a Gloucester Road
Bishopston
Bristol BS7 8BN
0117 924 1234
0117 944 1387

Office of Fair Trading
Public Liaison Unit
Field House
15-25 Breams Buildings
London EC4A 1PR
0345 224499 - consumer
information line
0171 269 8961

Mailing Preference Service
5 Reef House
Plantation Wharf
London SW11 3UF
0171 738 1625
0171 978 4918 - will remove your
details from the mailing list of its
licensed direct mail users

The National Newspapers' Mail
Order Protection Scheme Limited
(MOPS), 16 Tooks Court
London EC4A 1LB
0171 405 6806
0171 404 0106 - governs the mail
order industry. MOPS will
reimburse consumers who've lost
money as a result of the member
advertiser going into liquidation or
bankruptcy or ceasing to trade.

Radio Electrical and Television
Retailers' Association
Retra House, St. John's Terrace
1 Ampthill Street
Bedford MK42 9EY
01234 269110
01234 269609 (f)

Association of Manufacturers of
Domestic Electrical Appliances
Leicester House, 8 Leicester Street
London WC2H 7BN
0171 437 0678

The Office of the Banking
Ombudsman
70 Gray's Inn Road
London WC1X 8NB
0171 404 9944
0171 405 5052 (f)

National Consumer Council
20 Grosvenor Gardens
London SW1W 0DH
0171 730 3469

Consumers' Association
P O Box 44
Hertford X, SG14 1SH
01992 822800
0171 830 8585 (f)

The National Association of
Citizens' Advice Bureaux
115-123 Pentonville Road
London N1 9LZ
0171 833 2181
0171 833 4371

Chapter 2

Getting Good Service

We all have to buy services. Whilst they are not tangible or even edible as many of the goods are on the High Street, you can expect a reasonable standard of the person providing the service. For consumers the main problem is one of quality control. Goods are easy to complain about - mouldy fruit or a leaky pair of shoes are obvious. In most cases the retailer will be in no position to resist your complaint. But with services and tradesmen in particular, there is much more room for dispute. Remember that usually you won't have any knowledge or experience of the service you've bought into. If you've just had your house re-roofed and suspect a problem, how do you challenge a roofer who denies everything?

Services are often much more expensive than your High Street goods. This may mean a reluctance on the part of the service provider to accept a problem and the possibility of legal costs if you have to fight through the courts.

But you can help yourself. A little homework, forward planning and evidence gathering can avoid much long-term heartache and expense.

2.1 HOME IMPROVEMENT AND REPAIR
From roofers to decorators and from plumbers to electricians, you will have to call upon the services of a tradesman at some stage. But how do you find the right man for the job?

Personal recommendations
Ask family, friends, colleagues and even trustworthy people in the particular industry. Don't rely on Yellow Pages or other advertising.

Shop around
Get quotes from two or three tradesmen. Make sure however that you specify the same job so that the quotes are a fair comparison. The quotes should be free and given on a no-obligation basis.

Check insurance cover
Confirm that the tradesman concerned has adequate personal liability and property damage cover. If possible ask to see the relevant certificates. A tradesman who cuts corners with insurance is sure to cut corners in your home.

Inspect
If the tradesman has got nothing to hide, insist on seeing an example of his most recent work.

CASE HISTORY

Maria wanted a new conservatory in time for the summer. She didn't know anyone locally so she responded to a flyer from "DAC Construction" which had landed on her doormat the previous winter. Mr Callow from DAC provided an estimate on a scrappy piece of paper for "£5,000" but he failed to detail precisely what he would do for his money. Maria accepted his estimate and the work was started in March. By the end of July, the conservatory was still only half-built. Mr Callow stated that the materials had cost him more than he'd expected so he bullied Maria into parting with another £2,000. Either she paid or he'd walk off the job leaving the construction in a dangerous condition exposed to the elements.

The job was eventually "finished" in mid-August but it cost Maria another £1,500 to have several serious defects put right. Her garden had been ruined by DAC's workmen. But he carried no insurance, had a list of judgments against him and was generally better suited to the Wild West than West Croydon. Maria had learned a very expensive lesson.

⚖ TIPPING THE SCALES OF JUSTICE ⚖

Always get a full written quotation which clearly spells out the tradesman's obligations.

Quotes and estimates

There is some confusion over the definition of these words and their legal effect. Generally, a quote is intended to be a firm price. If a tradesman gives you a document with precise details of the work required and the costs associated, this should be the end of your financial obligation. If he underestimates the amount of work or materials needed, tough. That's his problem. An estimate is used as a rough guide to the likely costs. It cannot be relied upon. If you accept an estimate make sure you check with the tradesman regularly (as the job progresses), how much of your money has been spent. Ask to see receipts. To avoid being presented with shock bills, get a firm quote which specifies precisely the work to be done.

The agreement

Once you've picked the perfect tradesman to do the job in question, you need a contract of some description. It should note the parties to the contract, including the tradesman's name, address and telephone number. It should confirm the provisions upon which you agreed orally - what is to be done, how long it will take and of course how much it will cost. In particular, the agreement should specify;

A schedule
Estimated start and completion dates. If it's a big job there should also be target dates for the completion of certain works.

The financial niceties
Don't be shy about this. If everything is not absolutely clear in the beginning, your shyness could prove to be expensive. Always try to agree a flat fee. Under such an arrangement there is no room for hidden extras and the tradesman has an incentive to work quickly and efficiently.

Clearing up
Make sure any agreement contains a clause which makes the tradesman responsible for clearing away any refuse/debris. You should also insist that your home is left clean and tidy.

Guarantees
Try to get agreement on a guarantee period for the materials used and the quality of the workmanship.

Subcontracts
Many jobs require sub-contracted labour. For example if you're having an extension built, the main contractor may have to sub-contract the flooring work to an expert. The contract should make it quite clear that you have no legal relationship with any such sub-contractor and that it is the main contractor's responsibility to oversee all the work and to pay the sub-contractor.

CASE HISTORY
Mary agreed with a builder to have her garage roof repaired. She signed a written contract. The builder himself did all the structural work but had to call in a sub-contractor to apply the asphalt. Mary paid the builder a flat fee of £500 to have all the work done. The sub-contractor failed to turn up. But the builder wasn't interested. He told Mary to chase the asphalter personally. This was wrong. As Mary had agreed one contract with the builder she was able to sue him successfully for the cost of getting another asphalter in to complete the job.

Overseeing the work
You'll be able to avoid a lot of problems if you stay in contact with the tradesman and supervise the project every step of the way. You could even

check the materials and fixtures before they're installed. If problems develop later on at least you'll be happy that the raw materials themselves were not faulty.

Emergency work/call-outs

Of course you may be at the mercy of a tradesman at a time of crisis. For example, your bath floods and brings down the dining room ceiling. Finding a reputable tradesman, taking up references and checking his insurance cover is simply not an option.

But you can still protect yourself. You'll probably look for an emergency plumber/electrician/locksmith etc. in the Yellow Pages or local paper. If possible go for one of the household names like Dyno-Rod. If the company accepts credit cards you'll have valuable Consumer Credit Act protection (see previously).

Ask about charges. Look for a firm which doesn't charge a call-out fee. Agree the hourly or half-hourly rate before the contractor starts work. Ask to see his terms and conditions. Check the small print very carefully. If possible opt for a firm which is a member of one of the reputable trade associations. Always oversee the work - make sure that the work you're charged for has actually been done.

Your legal rights

The main legal weapon in the armoury is the Supply of Goods and Services Act 1982 (SOGSA). The law requires the work of the tradesman to be carried out to a reasonable standard.

⚖ TIPPING THE SCALES OF JUSTICE ⚖

SOGSA says that tradesmen must:
- *Carry out the work with reasonable skill and care.*
- *Do it within a reasonable time.*
- *Make a reasonable charge if no charge is agreed in advance.*
- *Use materials which are of satisfactory quality and fit for their purpose.*

The "reasonable standard" doesn't mean that you can expect all tradesmen to be gifted and the best at their job. It simply means an average standard according to the requirements of the work which you ask them to do. If your carpenter is a craftsman it's a bonus. If he's little more than a D-I-Y novice then he's not up to scratch.

If it becomes obvious mid-way through the work that he's not of a reasonable standard, don't suffer in silence and prolong the agony.

Pay him for the work which he's done which is acceptable and then sack him. Confirm all in writing. If you've paid all of the bill in advance (never a good idea, go for staged payments) then you'll have to threaten to sue to get your money back.

Always point out any defects as soon as they become apparent. Once the job is complete, it's often very difficult to get the tradesman back to carry out any repair works. If you're in dispute about the quality of the workmanship you may have to call in an expert or involve a trade association.

CASE HISTORY

Abi and Shaun had a new roof fitted. With the first heavy rain a leak was discovered. The roofer denied any responsibility. But as he was a member of the National Federation of Roofing Contractors (NFRC, see Databank) Abi and Shaun made a written complaint. The NFRC sent one of its inspectors to view the job. The roofer was found to be to blame and had to foot the repair bill.

So often the key to complaining successfully is evidence. If you have a good case in law you'll have to prove not only that the tradesman is at fault, but also your losses. Cases which may be weak on liability but which are otherwise well supported and evidenced can often succeed.

If the problem is not too severe, then you must give the tradesman the first opportunity to inspect and repair. Put him on written notice - detail the nature of the complaint and what you want done. Give a firm deadline.

If the threatening letter overleaf fails to do the trick then you may have to sue using the small claims court. Whilst litigation can be effective, it should be seen as very much a last resort. If you've done your homework early on and chosen a reputable tradesman/firm, then the chances are that you won't get yourself into too much of a pickle. But there are still too many cowboys operating.

Withholding payment

If you've got a problem, nothing focuses the mind more sharply than a withheld payment. If a percentage of the contract price is payable on completion, don't pay it if there are genuine defects. By the same token, if the work is satisfactory, pay on time. It's always sensible to retain goodwill - you never know when you may need it.

If you do withhold make quite clear in writing why you think that there's a problem and what needs to be done to put it right. Give a deadline. Don't sign a satisfaction note (a note to say that you're 100% happy with all the work) if you're in any doubt. If the tradesman refuses to do any work until he's been paid or threatens to leave the place in a real mess, you may have no alternative. In such a situation pay up but write on the final invoice/receipt, *"Paid under protest without prejudice to my legal position. I reserve my rights to take legal action"*.

Bangit, Sawit and Nailit   *22 Runway Avenue*
Independent Roofing Contractors   *The Airport Estate*
Pentonville   *Heathrow*
London N1

Dear Mr Nailit

22 Runway Avenue

You will doubtless recall fitting a new sound-proof roof to my home in April of this year. Sound-proof it is not. The noise from Heathrow Airport is now worse than ever. A friend of mine who is a roofer, has had a look and told me that you used the wrong materials.

I must therefore urge you to come back to my home and give your proposals to do the job properly. If I fail to hear from you within the next 14 days, I will ask Mr Slater to do the work and recover the costs from you, if necessary through the courts.

I look forward to hearing from you at your earliest convenience.

Yours sincerely,

cc. NFRC

Missed appointments

The washing machine breaks down. You call out an engineer who promises to call, "Sometime tomorrow afternoon". You have to take half a day off work. Of course the engineer fails to show. Can you claim compensation? The engineer (it could be the department store delivering a new suite of furniture, or a decorator etc.) is certainly in breach of your verbal agreement. But unless you made it clear at the time of booking his services that you would have to take time off work or otherwise incur a loss, it's probably not worth pursuing.

⚖ *TIPPING THE SCALES OF JUSTICE* ⚖

When making an appointment make it quite clear that if the tradesman fails to turn up without warning, and you suffer a loss, you'll be claiming compensation.

Trade associations/protection schemes/arbitration

If you find yourself in a deadlock situation, consider a trade association/arbitration scheme. Some governing bodies are very good and offer the consumer excellent protection. If you're buying double glazing for example, The Glass and Glazing Federation has real clout to intervene on your behalf. But it can only help if the double glazing firm is a member and to be a member requires evidence of quality and solvency etc. The cowboy operators won't be accepted. Some trade associations are considerably less effective.

The Federation of Master Builders for example is often seen as a sign of quality to many consumers. In fact, it can be largely toothless to fight on your behalf. The following should be considered:

Builders
1. Guarantee Protection Trust Ltd.
2. National Federation of Roofing Contractors.
3. National House Building Council.

Repairs/home improvement
1. Glass and Glazing Federation.
2. Institute of Plumbing.
3. National Association of Plumbing, Heating and Mechanical Services Contractors.
4. National Inspection Council for Electrical Installation Contracting.
5. The Decorators Association.

2.2 OTHER SERVICES

There are far too many services which we all buy into to be featured in any great detail in this volume. The following are perhaps the most commonly complained about.

Dry cleaners

Most people have a tale to tell about a shrunk or otherwise ruined favourite garment. To keep such wrangles to a minimum, the starting point is the garment care label. In the unlikely event that the garment doesn't withstand the care recommended by the manufacturer on the label, the retailer is liable for not selling goods of satisfactory quality.

Dry cleaners must exercise reasonable skill and take reasonable care of your garments. But mistakes are still made. As is so often the case, it is proving the cause of the defect which can be difficult. If the sleeve of your favourite linen jacket has a bleach mark when you collect it, who's to say it wasn't there before.

To minimise the risk of dispute;

- Check the garment carefully before you take it to the cleaners. Look for rips, tears and stains. Point these out to the cleaner.
- Check the garment carefully before you leave the cleaners. Point out any problems immediately.
- Look for a cleaner which is a member of the Textile Services Association. The TSA will put you in touch with an independent laboratory. An expert will then be able to decide if the cleaner is at fault. If it is, it'll have to pay you compensation and refund you the cost of the report.
- If the cleaner is not a TSA member you may have to go to court. Complain in writing before you do so and produce evidence to show how much the item will cost to replace.

Lost/stolen garments

Many dry cleaners send garments away to be cleaned by a central industrial unit. If your garments get lost in transit and you can prove that the cleaner failed to take reasonable care, you'll have a claim to compensation. Usually their replacement cost minus a sum to take account of fair wear and tear.

⚖ TIPPING THE SCALES OF JUSTICE ⚖

The law says that you can't be put in a better position than you were before the damage occurred. This is called betterment. If the only way to compensate you for a ruined cashmere sweater is to buy a new one, don't expect to get 100% of the asking price. The reduction will vary according to the age and condition of the damaged garment.

When you take a garment to a dry cleaner (or any other service provider) he is said to act as a bailee for value. You are called the bailor. If your garments are stolen whilst in the possession of the bailee, you won't automatically have a claim against him. You'll have to prove negligence - for example he failed to lock up his premises at night. If you can't establish fault then there is similarly no claim against his property insurance. You may however have cover as an extension to your own home contents policy. Check this with your broker/insurer - for a small amount, the extra cover can be invaluable.

In terms of damage to your garments, the dry cleaner (or indeed anyone acting as a bailee), may try to avoid their liability to you. The ticket you're given may state the terms and conditions upon which the work is undertaken. But such exclusion clauses are only enforceable insofar as they're fair and reasonable.

CASE HISTORY

Jean took her silk suit to the dry cleaners. She was given a ticket. On the back was printed, *"DNC Cleaners accept no responsibility for any damage howsoever caused. All garments cleaned at owners sole risk"*.

When she collected the suit, she discovered a big red stain on the skirt. The cleaner tried to rely on its exclusion clause. Jean sued. The District Judge found in her favour on two counts. Firstly, the terms and conditions were given to Jean *after* she agreed to have the work done and secondly, even if they'd been made clear before Jean agreed, they'd fail for being unreasonable.

Hairdressers

Anyone can set themselves up as a hairdresser. Tomorrow you could be let loose on the great British public armed only with a pair of scissors and a bottle of perming solution. Terrifying isn't it?

Of course most salons do have trained staff. But the level of training will vary enormously. A £20 perm may seem like good value. But if the hairdresser has only ever practised on a dummy or her boyfriend's grandmother you could be taking a big risk. The problem is knowing n advance whether the hairdresser is competent. Unless registered with the Hairdressers' Council, go with personal recommendations.

The following may also help;

- Inspect the salon personally. Speak with the preferred stylist.
- Look at the standard of cutting/colouring etc.
- Check to see if the salon is registered.
- Ask about prices in advance. There can be hidden extras - try to negotiate a fixed, inclusive price. Make sure unlimited coffee is included!

One of the principal complaints about hairdressers relates to damaged/discoloured hair. The stylist concerned has to take reasonable skill and care. They should quiz you about previous treatments and whether you've ever had a reaction to the chemicals. Always answer these questions truthfully. If you do have a reaction go and see your GP. In turn you may be referred to a dermatologist (skin expert) or trichologist (hair and scalp expert). If you've suffered badly, take photos, keep a diary of events and make a note of all your expenses. Notify the salon director immediately - let him see the damage but don't let him touch your hair. Confirm all in writing. You should then sue using the small claims procedure if your injuries aren't too bad. In all other cases, consult a solicitor experienced in personal injury work.

If the colour applied is wrong, again complain immediately. If the problem is obvious before you leave the salon, don't pay. In other cases speak with the boss as soon as you can. If the cut is poor or the perm has turned out looking like a crow's nest, again take photos and demand a refund and the cost of putting right the problem. If it's a real mess and you've no confidence in the salon, go elsewhere. You'll then have to recover the second fee from the original hairdresser/salon. This could be difficult. Avoid some of the anguish;

- Never go to a hairdresser and give the vague instruction to, "*do what you like with it!*"
- Have a clear idea of what you want done.
- Talk everything through with the stylist.
- Don't take in a photo of Cindy Crawford expecting to come out looking like her!
- Go for a Hairdressers' Council registered salon/stylist.

Removal firms
Moving home is quite stressful enough without having to worry about breakages and missing items.

It is important that you shop around to find a firm that you are happy with and offers adequate insurance. Again personal recommendations are probably the best. The firm will ask you to sign a contract. This will almost certainly contain terms and conditions seeking to either limit or exclude their liability in the event of breakages etc. Check the small print carefully. The terms must be fair and reasonable and will be subject to the Unfair Contract Terms Act 1977. In terms of the work of the removal firm itself, it must be to a reasonable standard under the Supply of Goods and Services Act 1982. So removers owe you a contractual duty, but also a duty of care in negligence. You can claim under either or both for losses and damage resulting from a lack of care. This will include the cost of repair, the cost of replacing lost items and reasonable redecorating costs if applicable.

The company concerned will almost certainly offer some form of insurance. This is probably a good buy provided you have read and understood all the policy stipulations (for example cover may be voided if you have interfered with the packing rather than leaving it to the "experts"). If insurance is offered, single liability for damage will be limited to a low figure. If you do not accept this you will have to fight out your case in court. Always look for firms which are members of the British Association of Removers. If both parties agree, it can appoint an independent arbitrator to consider the complaint and give a decision which is binding.

⚖ TIPPING THE SCALES OF JUSTICE ⚖

- *Check the small print.*
- *Take a full inventory of all your possessions.*
- *Let the removal firm do the packing.*
- *Check who's insured for what.*

Photo processing and photographers

Given the number of rolls of film which pass through the labs, the number of complaints is surprisingly small. But when it does go wrong, it can be an absolute disaster. Picking up someone else's holiday snaps can be quite amusing. Losing your wedding photos would not.

If you've got some very emotionally valuable photos to be printed, it's probably worth taking out extra insurance. In any event the processor will nearly always try to limit or exclude its liability to you. But again the terms must be properly communicated and they must be fair and reasonable. To doubly protect your position make clear how important the pictures are when you leave the film.

Try to use one of the larger more reputable processors. They tend to be bound by a code of practice and have guaranteed service standards. If your photos really are ruined or lost, be perseverant. Explain in writing why they would have been so valuable. Threaten to issue a court summons. In most cases, reputable firms will offer additional compensation. Choosing a photographer can be as risky as finding a good hairdresser. You can pay a lot of money for a finished product which leaves you feeling miserable.

1. Always go with personal recommendations.
2. Ask to see examples of the photographer's work.

3. Look for members of the British Institute of Professional Photography or the Master Photographers' Association
4. If you're having your wedding photos taken, make sure you know exactly what you're agreeing to. If you don't read the small print, you could find yourself contracted to a minimum number of expensive prints.

If you're unhappy with the prints and they're clearly badly lit or composed etc., you can insist on a re-shoot at the photographer's expense. But if the group wedding photos are a disaster this could prove a little difficult! In such a case, you'd have a claim to financial compensation.

⚖ *TIPPING THE SCALES OF JUSTICE* ⚖

Don't pay for all the photos up front. That way if they're not up to scratch, you can withhold a reasonable sum.

If the photos have simply not been printed very well, the photographer is obliged to arrange for a more acceptable set, all at his expense.

Chapter 2 - Databank

British Footwear Manufacturers
Federation
5 Portland Place
London
W1N 3AA
0171 580 8687
0171 580 8696

Glass and Glazing Federation
44-48 Borough High Street
London
SE1 1XB
0171 403 7177
0171 357 7458 - issues a Code of
Ethical Practice and runs a deposit
indemnity fund to protect
individuals contracting with GGF
members

National Federation of
Roofing Contractors Ltd.
24 Weymouth Street
London
W1N 4LX
0171 436 0387
0171 637 5215 - issues a Code of
Practice and offers a conciliation
and arbitration procedure

Building Guarantee Scheme (UK)
Ltd.,
143 Malone Road
Belfast BT9 6SU
01232 661717
01232 666323 - administers an
insurance backed guarantee to
customers of builders registered
with the scheme

Guarantee Protection Trust Ltd.
27 London Road
High Wycombe
Bucks HP11 1BW
01494 447049
01494 465194 - offers long term
insurance protection against
problems such as woodworm and
damp. The benefit is transferable to
new purchasers of your home. Only
members of the British Wood-
Preserving and Damp-Proofing
Association can offer GPT
guarantees

The Textile Services Association
7 Churchill Court
58 Station Road
North Harrow
Middlesex HA2 7SA
0181 863 7755/9177
0181 861 2115 - administers a
stringent Code of Practice to dry
cleaners who are members. Also
investigates complaints through its
customer advisory service

The Council for Registered Gas
Installers
4 Elmwood
Chineham Business Park
Crockford Lane, Basingstoke
Hants RG24 8WG
01256 707060
01256 708144 - will investigate
complaints against installers which
involve gas safety issues

Federation of Master Builders
Gordon Fisher House
14/15 Great James Street
London WC1N 3DP
0171 242 7583
0171 404 0296 - much vaunted
trade association but
serves it members more than the
public

National House Building Council
(NHBC)
Buildmark House
Chiltern Avenue
Amersham
Bucks HP6 5AP
01494 434477
01494 728521 - registers members
and issues the
excellent 10 year Buildmark
warranty to new homes

British Shoe Repair Association
10 Louvaine Avenue
Wickford
Essex SS12 0DR
01702 551566 - issues an oft
approved Code of Practice which
covers sales from shoe shops as
well as repairs. Also oversees a
complaints procedure

British Carpet Technical Centre
Wira House
West Park Ring Road
Leeds LS16 6QL
0113 259 1999
0113 278 0306 - runs an excellent
consumer complaints service
offering arbitration, mediation and

expert inspections. It's free to the
consumer even if the complaint is
not upheld

The Institute of Plumbing
64 Station Lane
Hornchurch
Essex RM12 6NB
01708 472791
01708 448987 - to be a member,
plumbers must meet exacting
criteria
and then be bound by its Code of
Professional Standards

The National Association of
Plumbing,
Heating and Mechanical Services
Contractors
Ensign House
Ensign Business Centre
Westwood Way
Coventry CV4 8JA
01203 470626
01293 470942

The British Decorators Association
32 Cotton Road
Nuneaton
Warwickshire CV11 5TW
01203 353776

The British Institute of
Professional Photography
2 Amwell End
Ware
Hertfordshire
SG12 9HN
01920 464011

The British Photographic
Association
Ambassador House
Bridstock Road
Thornton Heath
Surrey
CR7 7JG
0181 665 5395
0181 665 6447 (f)

Hairdressing Council
12 David House
45 High Street
London
SE25 6HJ
0181 771 6205
0181 771 3392 (f)

Institute of Trichologists
01625 862679

The Master Photographers'
Association
97 East Street
Epsom
Surrey
KT17 1EA
01372 726123

National Hairdressers' Federation
11 Goldington Road
Bedford
MK40 3JY
01234 360332
01234 269337 (f)

Chapter 3

Hotels And Restaurants

Staying in an hotel is a treat for many consumers. But for some, it's a way of life. The travelling salesman wants a comfy, quiet room at reasonable rates together with hearty food. A family taking a well-earned weekend break in the country may want four star luxury along with a pool and extensive leisure facilities. With both hotels and catering establishments, an element of "you pay's your money and take's your choice" is evident. But irrespective of the final bill there are minimum standards of service, quality and hygiene to be expected. If it all goes pear shaped, it's important to complain effectively.

3.1 HOTELS
Making a booking
Many people get a little confused when they book a hotel room. The fact is however that once you've made a booking, a binding contract has been entered into. This is the case whether you make the booking over the phone, in writing or in person. You may even be asked to leave a deposit. This is for two reasons - firstly, to confirm your intention and secondly, to compensate the hotelier if you cancel.

If you don't keep the booking, the hotel may either charge an amount to your credit card (if you've left a deposit this way) or even threaten to sue you. If you book with a central reservation service and secure the booking with a credit card, you'll be allowed to cancel the booking up to an agreed time without penalty. After that agreed time, be prepared to lose (at least) the deposit.

But hoteliers are under a strict duty to mitigate their losses. In simple terms this means that the deposit or other sum can only be withheld if the room has not been rebooked.

CASE HISTORY
Janice and Antonio booked a hotel for two nights for a weekend break. The booking was secured with a credit card and a £75 deposit taken. At 5 pm on the Friday, Janice developed a severe migraine and was unable to travel. The reservation had to be cancelled. Because of the short notice, the hotelier was only able to rebook their room for the Saturday evening. He was therefore entitled to keep the £75 deposit which represented his loss for the cancelled Friday booking.

Overbooking
This is a common problem in the hotel and leisure industry. But once you've made a firm booking, the hotel is contracted to provide the agreed facilities. If through its own mistake or underestimation of demand, you're left without a

room, you will be entitled to compensation. If you leave a deposit you'll get this back in full. You can also claim additional compensation for other losses arising as a direct result of the hotel being in breach. For example if the only comparable nearby hotel is more expensive you can claim for the difference plus the travelling expense.

But you too are under a duty not to exaggerate your loss. If the three star hotel is overbooked, don't check into the plushest 5 star London hotel and expect to recover all your losses!

To complain, write to the manager enclosing a copy of the booking reference. Attach copies of all relevant receipts etc., which prove your claim. If necessary, sue using the small claims court. If the hotel is a member of a chain or is represented by a single body, copy all the correspondence. If it's been misleading potential visitors or advertising services which don't exist, contact your local TSO.

Standards/service

If the hotel is of a lesser standard then can be reasonably expected, you're entitled to claim compensation. Also if the promised services aren't available, complain. If you plan a weekend break away on the promise of a heated pool and fully equipped gym, but neither is available, ask for a reduction in your final bill. The amount you can deduct will depend upon how much emphasis you placed on the particular service at the time of booking. If you're a travelling salesman who simply wants a place to rest your weary head, the unavailability of a gym probably won't be as important as a closed restaurant and bar.

If the hotel rooms are dirty or otherwise unhygienic, report the matter to the manager and your local Environmental Health Officer (EHO).

Stolen goods

You must take reasonable care of your possessions whilst staying at an hotel. Ideally, lock your valuables away in a safety box. Don't leave anything out on display. If you've acted in such a reasonable way but you still suffer a theft or damage to your possessions, then the hotel is liable. This is the goods news. The bad news is that provided the hotelier displays a disclaimer notice at reception his liability can be limited to £50 per lost item or £100 in total.

You can claim for your full loss if you can prove negligence on the part of the hotel or its staff. But this will be difficult. You'd have to show for example that the hotel failed to take reasonable precautions against such a loss.

CASE HISTORY

Kelly had her £650 video camera stolen from a hotel bedroom. The hotel denied liability and limited its loss to £50 relying on the disclaimer. But Kelly was very perseverant and asked a lot of questions. She discovered that a recently sacked housemaid had been allowed to keep her hotel keys. The police were called in to investigate. Because the hotel had been negligent in preventing such a loss, Kelly claimed successfully for the full amount.

⚖ TIPPING THE SCALES OF JUSTICE ⚖

Proving negligence against an hotel for stolen possessions is difficult. Take out household contents insurance which covers your belongings whilst away from home.

Hotel car parks

If you park in an hotel car park then you'll accept most of the risk. For example if it's stolen or broken into the loss will be borne by your insurance company. The only alternative is if the hotel has been negligent in some way.

CASE HISTORY

Murray parked in a Birmingham hotel car park. It was a hot summer's day so he opted for a spot under the shade of a tree. But the hotel failed to warn Murray that the tree concerned (which was on adjoining land) was due to be felled early the next morning. Murray's car was a write-off! Because the hotel had been negligent, he was able to claim against it for his uninsured losses, policy excess, loss of no-claim discount and hire car charges.

If you choose to park in an hotel car park when you're not a guest, don't be surprised to find your vehicle clamped. The Court of Appeal has approved of this practice provided:-

1. There are adequate warning notices.
2. The release fee is not exorbitant.
3. The clamp is released as soon as you show an intention to pay the fee. You have been warned!

Hotel bills

The presentation of your final bill can lead to one or two surprises. If you're at the front of a long line of impatient business travellers waiting to check out, complaining at the time can be embarrassing. To avoid such situations make sure when you check-in exactly what you'll be charged. Query if the rate you've been quoted for the room includes breakfast and VAT. Are there any other hidden extras? What is the hotel's charging policy on telephone calls? This can be very lucrative, so if you don't want a hefty bill, use a pay phone. What about the satellite TV channel - are the late night adult movies included? What about the mini-bar - are you used to paying £1.20 for a packet of crisps? If you've booked with a central reservation service, make extra sure that the price quoted is the price you'll pay.

Room service can be a costly luxury so again check the prices in the hotel directory carefully. A pint of beer (or any other drink for that matter) will generally cost more in an hotel bar than your local pub. If you're in for a session try to pay for the drinks as you go along with cash. If you sign a slip after every round there is room for error and confusion. The following morning you probably won't be able to remember accurately how much your party consumed - challenging a hefty bar bill will be difficult.

Accidents

The hotel is under a statutory (Occupiers' Liability Act) and common law duty to take reasonable physical care of its guests. If you fall down the stairs because they're slippery or because the handrail is inadequate you'll be able to claim financial compensation. But if the accident happens because your heels are too high, that's your problem. If you think that you're entitled to claim for personal injury, you have three years from the date of the accident. You'll probably need to enlist the support of a solicitor.

3.2 RESTAURANTS

There's no doubt that Britons now eat out far more regularly than at any other time. But we're hopeless at complaining about poor food and service standards. We're just too polite. The Americans and our EU counterparts, who have long been accustomed to eating out frequently, expect and generally receive, good service. In the UK waiting tables is seen as a dead-end job with poor prospects. Many waiters and waitresses take no pride in their work. Consequently we receive indifferent or even poor service.

Poor service - rights

If the service is not up to scratch, whether you can make a deduction from the bill depends upon the restaurant's service charging policy.

If a service charge is compulsory and automatically added to your bill (it must say so on the menu) you must pay it unless the service was unreasonable.

If the menu prices include service then you can deduct a sum of between 10 and 15% if the service was poor. Finally, if service is left at your discretion, don't leave anything!

Many people simply find the prospect of complaining in front of a restaurant full of diners too embarrassing. If you pay all the sums demanded and then try to complain a few days later, you'll be in a weak position.

⚖ TIPPING THE SCALES OF JUSTICE ⚖

Have a discreet word with the restaurant manager about the service out of earshot of the other diners. In nearly every case the manager will respond favourably and tell you not to leave a tip. He may even knock a bit extra off the bill or offer to buy a round of liqueurs etc.

There have been several attempts recently to simplify the restaurant service charge maze. The Consumers' Association has been campaigning to have service charges abolished altogether. Whilst no legislative changes are proposed, the Government is reviewing a 1988 Code of Practice which includes guidelines on restaurant service charges.

Cancelled bookings
If you make a booking for a table and don't keep it, the restaurant could sue for its losses. But the restaurant is under a duty to minimise its losses - during busy periods it's highly likely that the table will be taken by another party.

CASE HISTORY
Glenn and Paula booked a table for six for Paula's grandmother's 80th birthday. It was for a Monday night and a special menu had been created. About an hour before they were due at the restaurant, the old lady fell ill and the party had to be cancelled. The restaurant sent Glenn and Paula a solicitor's letter demanding its £200 lost profit - it had no other bookings that evening, had had to draft in extra staff and buy in special food. In these circumstances it was entitled to recover compensation.

Food poisoning
With more and more people eating out the scope for hygiene related problems increases. Whilst UK health and safety regulations are strict and stringently enforced, outbreaks of salmonella infection are on the up. If you become ill following a meal out you should contact your doctor - if you try to claim compensation later on, you'll need proof of your illness. You should also telephone your local Environmental Health Department. An officer may visit the restaurant and recommend prosecution. But you may be asked for a faecal sample to establish the precise type of infection. Keep a note of all your out of

pocket expenses - prescription charges, lost earnings, bus and taxi fares, special food etc. You should also keep a diary - note the days when you feel really ill. Then send all this information together with a doctor's letter to the restaurant. Its insurance company should make an offer in compensation. If you were very badly affected and perhaps even hospitalised the claim should be handled by a solicitor.

Accidents

These do happen in restaurants - people trip over chair legs, hands are cut on broken glasses and boiling soup can cause nasty burns. To succeed with a compensation claim you'll have to prove fault on the part of the restaurant (which will be liable for its employees) or another diner. Simple accidents aren't enough.

CASE HISTORY

John and Anya were at a function in a large restaurant. A band had been hired. One of the electric guitar cables hadn't been properly concealed so that when Anya got up to go to the loo, she slipped and broke her ankle. She succeeded in her compensation claim because the band had not taken proper precautions against such accidents and because the injury Anya sustained was reasonably foreseeable.

If a waiter spills food or drink on you, it would certainly be reasonable to expect the restaurant to pay dry cleaning charges - after all, he or she probably hadn't been taking proper care at the time.

Chapter 4

Holidays From Hell

From Blackpool to Barbados and from Ullapool to Utah the tourist's search for new destinations is shrinking the world. The once remote resorts populated exclusively by the rich and famous are now just a chartered Boeing ride away for us all. Latest figures show that more than 12 million Britons take an annual package holiday. Where Spain and the Balearic Islands were once the main destinations, today we're travelling to places more exotic and much further afield. The number of complaints is also on the increase. The travel industry of the past was often guilty of selling really shoddy holidays. Brochure wordings were regularly the subject of criminal proceedings and travellers often found themselves stuck in Spanish concrete jungles. Today, the industry is very heavily regulated and as such generally more honest. Tourists won't put up with sub-standard accommodation even at cut price rates. And in the generally more litigious mood of the late 1990's tour operators have to deliver the goods. But where is the line to be drawn? Is it fair to expect as much of a rustic holiday on a remote island in the Indian Ocean where the locals may have never seen Europeans as it is from a Majorcan sunshine fiesta? Necessarily an element of caveat emptor creeps in but the courts expect tourists to be reasonable. With this watchword in mind, this Chapter deals principally with disappointing package holidays. What can be expected, how to complain and when to let matters lie.

4.1 AGENT OR TOUR OPERATOR - WHO IS LIABLE?

Whilst many tourists do book direct with a tour operator, for example through Teletext, most people still use the High Street travel agent. In effect the agent is a holiday retailer. Because they don't physically sell the resort itself you'll be tempted by a bewildering array of glossy brochures each trying to get you to part with your cash. But make no mistake, once you book a package, your contract is with the tour operator, NOT the agent. So if you buy an Airtours Sundeal package to Majorca from Thomas Cook in Birkenhead and it turns out to be a disaster, it is Airtours which is obliged to offer compensation.

High Street agents or TV brokers etc. are really only agents of the tour operator. This confuses many holidaymakers because in nearly all other cases consumers' legal rights are enforceable against the High Street retailer, not the manufacturer.

If you buy a Sony hi-fi from Dixons, you'll be told that Dixons, as the retailer, must repair it or refund the purchase price. Everything changes with package holidays and unless the agent has misrepresented the holiday in some way, complain to the tour operator.

⚖ *TIPPING THE SCALES OF JUSTICE* ⚖

- *If you buy a package holiday, your contract is with the tour operator.*
- *The travel agent merely acts as a broker.*
- *Unless the travel agent misrepresents the holiday in some way, you'll have no claim if your holiday is a disaster.*

4.2 THE BROCHURE

The vast majority of holidays are chosen from the volumes of glossy brochures displayed seductively on travel agents' shelves. You pick a holiday, the travel agent taps in a code number on her computer and if there's room and airseats available, the holiday is booked. The brochure description and photographs are usually all that you'll have to make your decision. It's therefore critical that the brochure paints a fair and accurate picture of the resort and accommodation. If you're 2,000 miles from home it's often difficult to complain about a glamorous photo you saw in a travel agents one wet November day in Bolton.

In the past, tour operators tended to use very imaginative language. For high-rise block, 2 miles from the beach but ½ mile from the airport, read, "*Delightful architecture, excellent transport links, adjacent a fabulous long, sandy beach.*" Not surprisingly, there were many very disappointed tourists.

But just as estate agents' flowery language has been tightened up on house sale particulars, so the travel industry has come under close scrutiny from the legislators. The Package Travel, Package Holidays and Package Tours Regulations 1992 have, in many respects, revolutionised the way in which holidays are sold in the UK.

If a brochure contains misleading information, you have a legal right to claim compensation. But there can also be criminal liability. Where a brochure is made available to the public, it must contain legible, comprehensible and accurate information about specific aspects of the holiday including:

1. The destination and the means, characteristics and categories of transport used.
2. The type of accommodation, its location, category or degree of comfort and its main features.
3. Included meals.
4. The itinerary.

5. General information about passport and visa requirements which apply to British Citizens and health formalities required for the journey and the holiday.
6. Either the monetary amount or the percentage of the price which is to be paid immediately and the timetable for payment of the balance.
7. Whether a minimum number of people is required for the package.
8. The arrangements, if any, which apply if delayed at the outward or homeward points of departure.
9. The arrangements for securing of money paid over and for the repatriation of the holidaymaker in the event of insolvency.

A failure to give this information could lead to very costly court proceedings. There is additional protection found in the Trade Descriptions Act 1968. A false statement made by a tour operator in its brochure or by a travel agent could also lead to a criminal prosecution.

The Association of British Travel Agents (ABTA) own Tour Operators' Code of Conduct provides protection. ABTA represents 90% of tour operators and travel agents in the UK. The Code lays down the minimum standards of brochures requiring that they contain clear, comprehensive and accurate descriptions of things such as the means of travel, nature of accommodation and meal facilities offered. So if you've a complaint about a brochure or the way in which a holiday has been described, the law is there to help.

4.3 THE HOLIDAY CONTRACT
The Package Travel Regulations make virtually every statement in a brochure a term of your contract with the tour operator. This of course means that the operators are very careful about what they write.

Deciding on whether a contract has been made is really a matter of commonsense. If you're booking a holiday at a travel agent, the chances are that you'll sit in front of an on-line booking system and a rep will see if the holiday you've chosen from the brochure is available.

When you indicate that you're happy with the details and the agent presses a button on the computer, the contract is made. The only thing left to do is leave a deposit, or if you're within 8 to 10 weeks of the scheduled departure date, pay the full amount. If you're booking direct by phone often having seen brief "last minute" details on Teletext, the contract is made once you agree to the details offered by the telephone operator and give your credit card number.

Surcharges
Adding surcharges was often a painful financial burden. Both the Package Travel Regulations and the ABTA Code of Practice have quite a lot to say on

these charges. In essence, the brochure must make clear that the tour operator can only add a surcharge because of increased transportation costs, a change in the exchange rate or because of a variation in landing taxes etc. But no increases can be made less than 30 days before your holiday is due to start and the first 2% of any increase must be absorbed by the tour operator.

CASE HISTORY

Melvyn booked a £2,000 holiday to Kenya, seven weeks before he was due to depart. He paid the full price at the time of booking. The brochure, in its small print, reserved the tour operator's right to add fuel surcharges which were, *"due to market forces beyond the control of the company"*. Seven days before Melvyn was due to fly out to Nairobi, he received a demand for an extra £35 to cover increased aviation fuel prices. The tour operator told Melvyn if he didn't pay, they wouldn't release his tickets. But on his return to the UK, he sued the tour operator and won on two counts. Firstly, the surcharge was demanded within 30 days of Melvyn's departure and secondly, as the holiday cost £2,000 the operator should have borne the first £40 of any surcharge (i.e. 2%).

Insurance
There is no legal obligation to take out travel insurance. But it is of course very sensible to take out full cover. Many tour operators offer a discount on the package price on condition that you take out their insurance. This practice came in for some criticism as being unfair and unduly restrictive. But the bottom line is that a tour operator *can* insist on you taking out their insurance just like any other term of the agreement. The courts take the view that if you don't like one particular deal you're quite at liberty to walk away from it and straight into another travel agent.

Window price advertisements
"Caribbean Cruises from £59." Sounds tempting doesn't it? But is this holiday really available? By law, it should be. The travel agent's window may be the key to getting you to walk through the door. Holidays are very price sensitive. Whilst quality accommodation and daylight flights may be important, if the price is wrong, you won't book. So the agent will display a range of tempting deals to whet the appetite. The Trade Descriptions Act says that the prices advertised mustn't be misleading. So provided the holiday is available at the price advertised there will be no come-back against the agent. The ad need only say *"from £59"* etc. It would clearly be unreasonable to have to spell out the small print relating to every holiday.

If the holiday advertised is not available even if you do comply with all of the booking conditions, contact your local Trading Standards Office immediately. Try to take a photo of the advertised holiday.

4.4 AIR TRAVEL

When you book a package holiday, the air travel will be included. This means that you won't have to worry about booking with an airline and paying any extra. But the main drawback is that you'll be very much at the mercy of the airline and the tour operator. The smaller charter airlines in particular often change schedules at short notice and may be susceptible to technical problems and long delays. It goes without saying that an airline with three aircraft is unlikely to have any extra capacity to cover such eventualities. In 1996, 80% of scheduled flights left within 15 minutes of the listed departure time. But only 52% of charter flights could claim the same level of punctuality.

Also, with a package holiday it's unlikely that you'll be able to alter your travel arrangements - at least not without paying a heavy penalty. On the subject of ticket alterations, if you book direct with the airline, it's generally accepted that the cheaper the fare, the more restrictive the travel conditions will be. Fully flexible and fully refundable tickets are usually the domain of the business traveller as they don't come cheap!

What if the airline goes bust?

Summertime always brings horror stories of tourists stranded overseas as a charter airline or tour operator goes belly-up. But in most cases you should be OK. Always make sure that the tour operator has an ATOL licence. The booking form/invoice will carry the ATOL logo and certificate number. This is the Civil Aviation Authority's guarantee that;

1. If the tour operator goes bust before your holiday starts you'll get your money back or;
2. If it happens whilst you're away, you can finish your holiday and be transported home by another airline without any extra cost to you.

CASE HISTORY

Philip and Ceri were always on the look-out for a bargain. So they were chuffed to get on a two week package to Majorca with "Manana Holidays" for £129 each. But ten days into the trip they read in the English newspapers that the company had collapsed leaving massive debts and around 10,000 tourists stranded in various sunshine resorts. But it got worse - because Manana didn't have an ATOL licence and as Philip and Ceri hadn't taken out extra insurance, they had to pay to get home on a scheduled airline. Their corner-cutting ended up by costing them an extra £280 each. Ouch!

⚖ TIPPING THE SCALES OF JUSTICE ⚖

- *Be wary of bargain-basement packages - the cheaper the deal the more likely it is that corners will have been cut.*
- *Always look for an ATOL licence.*
- *Always pay by credit card - if the airline or tour operator fails the card issuer is obliged to refund the costs of getting you home.*
- *Always take out extensive travel insurance.*

Passports/visas
Don't rely on the word of a travel agent or a friend. Always check with the relevant Embassy etc. to see what is required. It is solely your responsibility and if you turn up without a visa don't be surprised if some countries put you on the first flight home.

Health/inoculations
Again this is the traveller's responsibility. Most holiday brochures will give some guidance, but if in doubt speak with your GP. Better still, obtain a copy of the booklet *Health Advice for Travellers* from The Post Office.

Luggage
Considering the millions of suitcases that travel the world every day, the number which get damaged or lost is minute. But if it happens to you, it can be devastating. The contents of a suitcase are incredibly personal but the airline is unlikely to show any concern. Always check that your travel policy has baggage cover. Some don't.

When you check in you'll be given tags for the baggage. Don't lose these. They are the airline's way of tracing lost items. As soon as you realise that you have a problem, report it to the airline's ground handling agent. You'll be asked to complete a Property Irregularity Form (PIR). In most cases you will be reunited with your luggage within a couple of days. If you have to buy essential items in the meantime, either the airline concerned will pay compensation or you can claim on your travel policy. Always keep receipts. If the bags simply never turn up, the airline has to pay compensation. But the bad news is that the amount is based on the weight and not the contents of the missing luggage. Don't expect to recover any more than £250 - 300. These limits are set by the Warsaw Convention.

Delayed/cancelled flights

Delayed flights are an everyday part of air travel. It is very seldom that an aircraft, particularly those operated by charter airlines, take off precisely on time. The tour operator is actually under no legal obligation to provide refreshments or accommodation in the event of delay. But if it does, it must make it clear in the brochure. So if you end up spending the night on an airport floor along with 300 others, there is no comeback on either the airline (if scheduled) or the tour operator. But you should be able to claim a paltry amount from your travel insurers - typically £20 after the first 12 hours. If delayed by more than 24 hours the policy should entitle you to claim a full refund. Again, the importance of travel insurance is emphasised.

Overbooking

This problem is unlikely to affect tourists on charter flights. If you're travelling independently or on a scheduled airline you may find that there aren't enough seats on the aircraft. Airlines routinely overbook to allow for cancellations - but sometimes they get it wrong. Provided you have a valid ticket and check in on time, you're entitled to cash compensation. Usually airlines bend over backwards to get you on the next flight or if necessary will put you up in very good accommodation. When you do get on a flight, with a few extra quid in your pocket, always ask for an upgrade.

On-board safety/behaviour

The Captain of the aircraft is legally entitled to refuse entry to anyone he considers incapable of flying. So don't get too drunk! Also, rowdy and drunken behaviour in-flight can lead to the plane being diverted. Not only will you be met off the aircraft by the local police, but you could get a nasty bill from the airline.

You should always familiarise yourself with the airline's safety procedures and if the Captain asks you to put on your seat belt, do it. Passengers injured whilst flying through turbulence but not wearing their belts when asked to do so, haven't been allowed to claim compensation.

Complaints

Complaints about airlines are commonplace. They range from gripes about leg-room, to dirty toilets, to not being able to see the movie screen to snoring passengers. But for the most part, they're not very serious and are usually met with polite letters from the airline and perhaps a voucher towards the cost of the next ticket. But on occasion they can be worth pursuing. If you're struck down with food poisoning, you should complain.

Similarly, passengers get hit by items falling from overhead lockers. If you can show that the cabin crew knew or ought to have known of the risks or had failed to warn properly what could happen, again, complain. Also if a stewardess spills hot coffee on you or trips you up with the trolley, it's certainly worthwhile submitting a formal claim.

⚖ TIPPING THE SCALES OF JUSTICE ⚖

- *Report your complaint to the on-board crew. Take the name of the pursar or chief stewardess.*
- *Ask for the address of the airline's customer service department.*
- *Try to get the details of any fellow passengers who are similarly affected or who can act as witnesses.*
- *If you're injured, or ill, ask to see the hospital doctor on arrival.*
- *Always keep receipts of all expenses and if your illness is on-going keep a diary of events.*
- *Always complain in writing - quote the airline's reference.*
- *If necessary, be prepared to see a solicitor.*

4.5 COMPLAINTS ABOUT YOUR HOLIDAY
At the resort
There is most definitely a correct way to complain about a poor holiday. Haphazard, poorly evidenced and supported and vague complaints are unlikely to be taken too seriously. If you're on a package trip, the complaint is likely to be about either the accommodation, the facilities, the food or the resort in general (or a combination of all). Most tourists want to enjoy their hard-earned break and aren't initially too bothered about compensation. It's therefore critical to complain early.

⚖ TIPPING THE SCALES OF JUSTICE ⚖

Effective complaining;
1. *Find the tour rep. Complete a written complaint form.*
2. *If the accommodation is not up to scratch, demand to be moved. If the food is atrocious demand cash compensation to pay for meals at local restaurants.*
3. *If the rep seems helpless or not interested phone the tour operator in the UK and speak with a manager. Repeat your demands - tell them if they don't co-operate and get your*

holiday back on track they'll be hearing from your lawyers.
Get a receipt for the cost of the phone call.
4. *Get evidence. Take photos, videos, sound recordings. Take the*
   details of witnesses. If necessary complain on a joint basis -
   the more of you that shout, the greater the chances of
   something being done.
5. *Don't suffer in silence. If you try to complain when back in*
   the UK, the tour operator will need to know how your holiday
   was affected.
6. *If the problem is ongoing and cannot be resolved (perhaps a*
   noisy hotel), keep a diary of the disturbance.
7. *Keep receipts for all out of pocket expenses.*
8. *Be reasonable and polite. Don't expect as much from a £99*
   last minute bargain in unnamed accommodation as from a
   £2,000 break in a platinum coast hotel in Barbados. Different
   countries have different standards so don't expect your
   holiday to be the same as 2 weeks in the UK. Be tolerant but
   complain where you've clearly been let down.

Back in the UK

Chances are that if you complained early enough and to the right person, most of your gripes will have been remedied whilst overseas. But if not you'll have to follow up a complaint with the tour operator. Your claim is likely to be for the loss of enjoyment suffered as a result of problems with the holiday.

CASE HISTORY

Stuart and Betty are keen divers. They booked a package to Israel that included diving trips to the Red Sea. But on arrival, the diving operator proved to be rude and aggressive, his equipment was dangerously out of date and the promised spectacular dives never materialised.

On their return to the UK Stuart complained in writing with evidence of their disappointment. At first they were offered £100 each (the holiday had cost £399 per person). They rejected this and threatened court proceedings. Stuart argued that the very reason they'd booked the holiday was for the diving - a fact made quite clear to the tour operator. On this basis the tour operator reconsidered its position and offered a full refund of the holiday price.

Generally, tour operators will not offer full refunds - their argument is that in spite of problems with the holiday, you would have got some benefit and enjoyment. This is a difficult argument to counter although the first offer should usually be rejected. After all, the tour operator will try to get away with paying the bare minimum.

There is absolutely no point in pursuing a complaint solely on a point of principle. You need hard evidence and you need to show that the complaint is reasonable. If most tourists would have accepted the arrangements and adopted a "let's make the most of it" approach, then the tour operator won't be impressed by whingers.

But do try to have in mind a figure which you would accept in compensation. In addition to recompense for out of pocket expense, if half the holiday was ruined, insist on half your money back. If the problems were less serious, perhaps £50 per travelling passenger would suffice.

Once you've entered into negotiations, don't regard it as some kind of game. If the tour operator sends a cheque for £25 return it immediately or bank it and write back saying that it's been accepted in part settlement. But only do so if you've got a good claim and you use it as an opportunity to resolve the dispute quickly.

⟦⟧ *TIPPING THE SCALES OF JUSTICE* ⟦⟧

1. *If you're claiming compensation for injuries don't settle until you're sure that you've made a full recovery. Once you accept an offer "in full and final settlement" you'll lose the right to go back for more.*

2. *Under The Package Travel Regulations you can now hold the UK-based tour operator responsible for injuries sustained at foreign hotels - provided you can prove some fault (for example a floor left dangerously slippery). In the past tourists would have had to sue the hotel proprietor directly, usually in a foreign court.*

4.6 GOING TO COURT

In most cases, you'll be able to resolve your complaint with a few letters. But if the tour operator flatly denies responsibility or doesn't offer sufficient compensation, you're effectively left with two options.

The ABTA Arbitration Scheme

The Chartered Institute of Arbitrators administers this on behalf of ABTA. Awards of up to £1,500 per passenger or £7,500 per booking can be made against the tour operator.

If you're in a deadlock situation with the tour operator, you'll need to send in full written particulars to ABTA together with a small registration fee. A file of papers is then submitted to an independent arbitrator (your complaint, the tour operator's "defence" and your comments on the "defence"). All supporting documents should of course be submitted (keep copies). Because the arbitrator makes his decision without hearing oral representations, it is very important to paint a fully descriptive picture of the complaint. For this reason, complex cases which require explanation in person should not be referred to the ABTA scheme. Personal injury claims are excluded.

The Award of the Arbitrator is binding on both parties. Once you've agreed to this you lose the right to go to court. But the Award itself can be enforced just like any other judgment through the courts.

Pros

- Quick, straightforward, reasonably cheap.
  - No fear of going to court.
  - Binding on the ABTA member.
  - Expensive for the tour operator.

Cons

- May be difficult to properly convey the emotional aspect of a disappointing holiday.
  - Awards can be on the low side.
  - Decision is binding.

The Small Claims Court

A Small Claims Court doesn't actually exist. What we have is a procedure of the county court which deals with small claims. Small claims are currently those up to £3,000 (£1,000 in the case of personal injuries).

Going to court is a prospect which terrifies many. Lawyers are expensive, delays are commonplace and Legal Aid isn't generally available. And if you lose, you'll have to pay not only your costs, but those of the other side too. These are all true of the county court proper, but the small claims/arbitration procedure (don't confuse this with ABTA's) can, if used properly, provide a relatively painless way of suing.

The basis of the procedure is that no costs are awarded - even if you lose. So, unless you're prepared to pay for a solicitor privately, most people will appear unrepresented. The procedure is designed to be user-friendly and a range of free booklets explain all that you should need to know. There are no complex rules of procedure and evidence and the District Judge has a wide discretion to hear or see whatever evidence he likes. You may not even have to take the oath.

The only cost you'll have is the summons issue fee - £10 - £80 depending on the value of the claim. But you'll get this back if you win. To issue the summons you'll have to complete one of two forms, either N1 or N2.

If you're claiming a fixed sum, for example the cost of the holiday plus your out of pocket expenses, use form N1. But if you're claiming a sum for general distress, inconvenience and disappointment, you'll need to use form N2. Don't ask for a specific sum but simply "Damages to be assessed". Rather than use the small space on the form to describe your holiday, it's a good idea to submit separate particulars. An example is overleaf.

Pros

- The threat of litigation can be a powerful negotiating tool.
- Procedure is simple and cheap.
- No fear of paying lawyers costs, even if you lose.

Cons

- Delays can run into many months.
- Fear for some of appearing in court.
- If you have to pay for expert evidence or witnesses you'll only be able to recover a proportion of the fees.

There are other trade associations and mediation services which can offer assistance. The Association of Independent Tour Operators for example represents more than 150 specialist tour operators. It offers an Independent Dispute Settlement Service very similar to ABTA's arbitration scheme.

IN THE REDHILL COUNTY COURT

Case No:

B E T W E E N:

Duncan Callow   *Plaintiff*

and

Sunshine Disaster Tours Limited   *Defendant*

PARTICULARS OF CLAIM

1. The Plaintiff booked a holiday to The Apartments Playa del Gringos ("the apartments"), Tenerife with the Defendant. The inclusive price for four adults on half board basis was £1,499.
2. On arrival, the apartments were unavailable. The Plaintiff was kept waiting at Tenerife airport for 6½ hours whilst alternative accommodation was sought. No refreshments were made available.
3. Eventually accommodation was found in the North of the Island, approximately 25 miles from the resort originally booked with the Defendant. The Plaintiff had to pay for a private taxi to transfer them to the Hotel Esmerelda.
4. The accommodation at the Esmerelda was inferior - four adults had to share one room, the air conditioning did not work, there was no hot water and the swimming pool was closed for 10 of the 14 days. Only breakfast was provided although the Defendant had sold the holiday on a half-board basis.
5. Being at the North of the island, the resort was often shrouded in cloud. The Plaintiff had to take a taxi ride to the South coast beaches in order to see the sun.
6. By reason of the matters aforesaid, the Plaintiff has suffered loss:

Essential refreshments at the airport	£15
Taxi fare to Hotel Esmerelda	£12
Daily return taxi fare to the beach	£120
Evening meals x 4 x 14	£560
Taxi fare to the airport	£10
	£717

7. Further the Plaintiff claims damages to be assessed to reflect the disruption, distress and inconvenience caused to the Plaintiff and his companions.

Dated:

Signed:

4.7 INSURANCE CLAIMS

Always, always, always take out full travel cover. Paying anything from £17 to £60 may seem like a waste of valuable holiday money. But if you're taken ill, lose your baggage or face long departure delays, it could be the best spend of your life. Of course you could fall into the category of always taking out a policy and claiming whenever possible "otherwise it's just a waste of money." But fraudulent claims cost us all because insurers have to increase the premiums. It's also a criminal offence.

But do make sure that you check the level of cover. Ensure that the policy covers all the members of your party. Check the period of insurance - if you're flying back overnight, you'll be a day late into the UK. You need to be covered until you and your baggage are safely home. Also consider the small print very carefully. Look to see on what basis your losses will be reimbursed - if it's on an indemnity, then allowance will be made for wear and tear. If it's new for old, expect to pay slightly more. There's also the excess to consider on each successful claim.

⚖ *TIPPING THE SCALES OF JUSTICE* ⚖

When claiming, be honest, reasonable and accurate. Insurers take a very hard line and require proof of losses;

1. *Always document delays, losses, accidents and thefts.*
2. *If in doubt always report accidents and thefts to the relevant authorities/police.*
3. *Get a record or crime reference number. Be perseverant, even if there is a language problem!*
4. *Always keep receipts for cash and travellers' cheques.*
5. *Don't take valuable photographic and electrical equipment with you unless you have the original proof of purchase.*
6. *Check that the insurance policy covers expensive video cameras etc. for their full replacement value.*
7. *Don't rely on the protection offered by credit/charge cards - the cover is usually very limited.*
8. *Keep the claim simple.*

Chapter 4 - Databank

Air Transport Users Council
5th Floor
Kingsway House
103 Kingsway
London WC2B 6QX
0171 242 3883
0171 831 4132 (f)

Association of British Travel Agents
55-57 Newman Street
London W1P 4AA
0171 637 2444
0171 637 0713 (f)

ATOL
Civil Aviation Authority
45-49 Kingsway
London WC2B 6TE
0171 832 5620

Association of Independent
Tour Operators (AITO)
133a St. Margaret's Road
Twickenham
Middlesex TW1 1RG
0181 744 9280

Chapter 5

Buying A Car

Buying a car has been described as more painful than a visit to the dentist. The motor trade can be pitiful - complaints about poorly prepared vehicles, overcharging, misrepresentation and appalling customer service are commonplace. It is rare indeed to hear of a pleasurable experience when buying a car. This must change! There are a few signs of improvement. Many manufacturers have revamped their customer service departments and the likes of Ford's Commitment scheme do help disgruntled consumers. But there's a long, long way to go, particularly when buying a used car. Given that a car is probably the single most expensive item you'll buy (aside from a house), it's important to know your rights.

But even when buying a used car the situation differs according to from whom the car was bought. With a private sale, that is from someone who does not deal in cars, even on a small-scale, the maxim, "let the buyer beware" is very much to the fore. Protection is scant and unless you have been specifically misrepresented about a particular aspect of the car, you'll be left to hold the baby, no matter what condition it's in.

5.1 BUYING USED FROM A DEALER

If you buy from a motor trader, the Sale and Supply of Goods Act 1994 (SSGA) applies. But many dealers are reluctant to accept that you have any rights at all and will try to sell to you on the basis of a trade agreement. If they tell you that it is, "sold as seen" or because of a, "vast discount" being offered you have effectively waived your consumer protection rights, do not worry. If you're a private purchaser the dealer cannot avoid the statutory protection afforded to you by the SSGA.

The whole used car trade has a somewhat tarnished image not helped by media portrayal. But many dealers are however, quite reputable and will do what they can to ensure that you drive away happy. Much of the problem actually stems from purchasers' unreasonable expectations. If you buy a high-mileage, rather sorry car for £500 from a dealer (whose profit margins may be negligible), do not expect years of luxury trouble-free motoring.

Obviously you will get what you pay for and the standard to be expected of the dealer will be commensurate with the age, price paid and mileage recorded on that car. In general, if you buy a car from a dealer, the SSGA requires that it:

1. Fits its description - i.e. the year or make and specification.
2. Be of satisfactory quality - again dependent upon the market at which the car is aimed and its price.
3. Be fit for its purpose.

If when you buy the car it falls down on one of these points, you must reject it immediately and seek a refund. The law allows only a short period for rejection because cars being the complex machines that they are means that there is ample scope for interference once away from the dealer. If you are buying a relatively high value car, it may be prudent to have it checked by an authorised engineer before it leaves the showroom. The time for rejection is critical and may have expired before you even realise that you have a problem. In practice, rejecting a car and claiming a refund is notoriously difficult. The courts struggled with the old concept of merchantability and took the view that in most cases as a car is merely a mechanical object it was always capable of repair.

Therefore if you are too late to reject your car or have a less than watertight case, your remedy instead will be to claim financial compensation - usually the cost of repair. You will also be entitled to claim for any reasonably incurred losses which arise as a result of your car being off the road.

Once your car has developed a problem, you should give the garage which sold it the first opportunity of repair. If it is something as major as a new gearbox, then it may be unreasonable to expect the garage to foot the entire bill. Every case will turn on its own facts and it is therefore difficult to generalise.

If you bought a £45,000 Ferrari from a specialist dealer, then you would not expect the gearbox to fail within a reasonable period of time. If it fails on a £250 1980 Mini, then you will have to pay a proportion (perhaps the larger part) of replacement costs.

If the garage has had several attempts at repairing your car but is either unhelpful or unwilling to eat into its profit margin, then you may consider taking the car elsewhere for repair. Again this decision will depend upon the particular circumstances of each case. The risk with such a course of action is that you will be lumbered with a second repair bill. It is unlikely that the first garage would welcome payment of it with open arms so you will be left with the threat of having to sue to recover.

To do so you will need to be sure of your evidence -the word of one garage mechanic against that of another will not suffice. You would probably need to enlist the support of an *independent* expert. Again this will incur additional cost - however you should be able to add this on to the total claim.

⚖ TIPPING THE SCALES OF JUSTICE ⚖

When buying from a dealer you should exercise caution. There are bargains to be had, but there are equally many rogue cars on the road;

- *Look at the car carefully - do the doors hang properly?*
- *Are there signs of filler or overspray?*
- *Check the tread on the spare tyre, turn on the ignition and ask a friend to see what comes out of the exhaust - a big blue plume could be the sign of a decidedly unhealthy engine.*
- *Does the engine itself look as if it has done the mileage indicated on the odometer?*
- *Check the service documents - a car with a bona fide service history has a definite advantage.*
- *If previous MOT certificates are available, scrutinise them to check that alleged mileages tally.*

The best advice is probably to walk away from any car or deal with which you feel uneasy. It is very easy to be sold a car in the comfort of a showroom. Do not be afraid to sleep on your decision, to shop around and to check that you can actually afford the car.

5.2 THE NEW CAR

New car buying has been called, 'the battle of the liars', with the better liar getting the best deal - usually the professional salesperson. But whether buying from a prestige dealer or from under the arches, your rights are exactly the same. We've already seen the three principal requirements, but trying to define what they mean could fill a volume in its own right, so here are two examples to illustrate the points.

CASE HISTORY

Mr Pearce bought his wife a new supermini. Within three weeks, the paint was flaking off the bonnet and a rear panel. The quality of the paint was clearly below par and, because the Act says that minor defects such as paint can be taken into account when considering satisfactory quality, he was entitled to a new car.

CASE HISTORY

Mr Johnson wanted a car capable of towing a caravan. He fancied a Rover 825 SLD and made this specific requirement known before he paid his deposit. However, before he took delivery, Rover's technical department told him that because the car had air-conditioning, the power unit wouldn't be fit for all the purposes specified. In this case, towing a caravan. Mr Johnson got his deposit back and walked away from the contract without penalty.

Changing your mind

Once you've signed an agreement to buy a new or used car, the contract is binding. If you change your mind or realise you can't afford it, be ready to lose at least the deposit. Hardline dealers could even threaten to sue for lost profit on the sale, especially if the car has been individually specified and proves difficult to sell to someone else.

CASE HISTORY

Mr Freeland signed up for a new Mazda MX5. He was recently retired and looking for a fun car, but when he got home he thought he'd made a mistake and would look foolish in it. He wanted out. But once his lawyer advised him he'd lose the deposit he didn't take much persuading to buy the car and enjoy every minute behind the wheel. He was, however, rather thankful he hadn't ordered a superbike - his original intention.

Delivery delays

Many standard order forms use a term that states, *'time for delivery of the car is not of the essence of the contract'*. If, when you place the order, you don't make clear any special reason why the car must be delivered by a specified date, you cannot cancel the agreement if delivery is delayed. But if the car is not delivered within a 'reasonable' period, write to the dealer and impose a deadline. Mention that if the car is not delivered within a week of your deadline you are entitled to treat the contract as null and void.

Who can you blame?

If the car fails to satisfy your expectations and you have a good case for replacement, refund or compensation, you have to claim against the dealer concerned. Although the manufacturer may be calling the shots, don't be fobbed off - your contract is with the dealer. It is he or she who is responsible in law for your problem.

If the car is riddled with faults, you can reject it, get your money back and claim compensation for reasonable losses. Or you can simply claim compensation - usually the cost of putting the car right. This is all much easier said than done: the dealer may argue that you've accepted the car and therefore lost your right to reject. The law says that you accept goods after a 'reasonable' period of time. But it fails to define how long 'reasonable' could be. Every case turns on its own facts.

CASE HISTORY

Mr Thomas bought a new Nissan Micra in October 1996. One of the doors was badly fitted and in need of replacement. Part of the car would also need a respray. Clearly it was not of satisfactory quality. But because he'd had the car for four months and covered 6,000 miles, the court ruled that he'd accepted it. Although not entitled to his money back, he could insist on a factory standard repair. The case cost him nearly £2,000 in legal fees, however. A sharp reminder of the risks of litigation.

5.3 WARRANTIES

All manufacturers now offer warranties. But remember, that like the information on a Mars bar wrapper, *'this does not affect your statutory rights'*, and the protection is merely in addition to your legal rights.

If you buy a car whose warranty has expired, the dealer may offer you mechanical breakdown insurance (MBI) for an annual premium. This, too, can provide valuable protection, but like most types of insurance it has its drawbacks. Always check the policy carefully. To qualify you'll probably need to have the car regularly serviced. Fair wear and tear of the major moving parts will usually be excluded.

5.4 STOLEN CARS

If buying from a dealer you can request an HPI check for £28.50. This is a register which contains details of stolen and written off cars and also those subject to finance agreements. It is not foolproof however and may not always be available. If you buy privately, there is always the risk that the car is stolen. Again a call to HPI may prove invaluable. You can probably never avoid this risk altogether, but common-sense will help. Check that the seller's name tallies with that on the vehicle's documents.

- Does the place of sale correspond with the address on the Vehicle Registration Document (V5)?
- Does the seller appear to know everything about the car or does he seem rather vague?
- Do you generally have a bad feeling about the seller?

Again, if in any doubt, walk away. What may seem like the bargain of the decade may be further evidence that the car has been stolen.

If you do go ahead and buy a car which subsequently turns out to be stolen, be prepared for a long, frustrating and expensive period. You never get a good title to a stolen car even if you have supposedly bought in good faith. You simply have no rights over the car which is still the property of the original owner or his insurer if he has already been paid out under a claim. The police or the insurance company may seize the vehicle and either return it to its lawful owner or place it in a police pound pending court action. Your remedy will be against the person who "sold" you the car for a full refund. If he too had been previously duped, then a chain will develop with each respective party claiming off the other. If the seller was the thief himself, then you can probably assume that you will be heavily out of pocket. If he is traced and prosecuted then there is the possibility of a compensation order being made in your favour. You could also consider the possibility of a private civil action against him like any other debt. But don't expect too much. If you do buy privately get as much detail about the seller as you can and avoid paying by cash.

5.5 CLOCKING

If the car bought has a false mileage reading and there was no sticker on the windscreen warning that the odometer may be wrong, you may have a claim for both misdescription and misrepresentation. It is a criminal offence for a dealer to make false statements about the cars they sell - including mileage. Prosecutions are brought by the Department of Trade and Industry under local Trading Standards Officers - the threat of such action may prove crucial in your claim for compensation. There are tell-tale signs. For example;

* Is the wear and tear on the foot pedals, seats, and gear selector etc. consistent with the purported mileage?
* Do the numbers on the odometer all line up?
* Does the fascia looked scratched or are the screws missing or damaged?

If you do buy a car which you can prove to have been clocked, then your remedy will usually be in the form of financial compensation: the true value of the car against the purported value when clocked.

5.6 RINGING

This is the process whereby stolen cars are given a new identity from written-off or scrap vehicles. The crucial part from a write-off - the vehicle identification number plate -VIN- is removed enabling the villain to obtain duplicate paperwork from the DVLA. A similar car is then stolen to order and after a brief spell in the workshop during which the VIN plates are exchanged and chassis/engine numbers ground down and replaced - miraculously a dead car is reborn. Again a check on the HPI register should avoid this risk but in any event check that all the paperwork tallies and look at the VIN plate carefully. There will usually be signs of force/scratches or the wrong-sized rivets.

5.7 RIGHT OF LIEN

If you take your car in for repair at a garage, it will exercise its right of lien over your car. In essence this means that it can lawfully hold on to the vehicle until its fees have been paid. If you dispute the sum or the work done, the only way to secure the release of the car may be to pay under protest without prejudice to your legal rights, and reserve the right to pursue legal remedies in due course. It may be sensible to write that you pay "under protest" on the invoice. In legal terms, stopping a cheque after the event cannot be condoned - for practical purposes such a course of action may prove highly effective.

5.8 BUYING AT AUCTION

In purchasing a new car you may consider a visit to your local auction house. Buying at auction has become an increasingly popular pastime and as it forms an intrinsic part of a car dealer's life, there are undoubtedly bargains available to the private purchaser. But there are also dangers.

The auctioneer can contract out of his SSGA responsibilities (e.g. satisfactory quality etc.) so you must read the auction particulars very carefully. If as is likely, the auction does not afford you any statutory protection, then the sale will not be a "consumer sale" and you will be largely responsible for any problems with the vehicle. It is therefore very important that you check the car, preferably with an expert, before you start bidding. A bright and tidy saloon may appear as the bargain of the century but in fact turn out to be a real dog. If in doubt, walk away.

Note also that until the auctioneer brings his hammer down on the deal, you can retract your offer.

5.9 FUNDING A CAR PURCHASE

A car is usually the second most valuable possession people own. But who really owns these cars? Often you may buy a car not with your own cash. If for private use, the money will often be supplied by a third party or by the dealer himself. The form of credit may be a loan, hire purchase, credit sale or conditional sale - all regulated, to a lesser or greater degree, by the Consumer Credit Act 1974.

If you buy with a loan, either privately from your bank or building society or from a finance company the dealer has introduced, you effectively buy with cash and the implied terms of the Sale and Supply of Goods Act, viz. satisfactory quality etc., will apply. If your car proves defective then you will be in no more secure a position than a pure cash buyer. However, if the loan is made by a connected lender such as a finance company introduced by the dealer, then under S.75 of the Act, you also have rights against this finance company. There are conditions attached to this valuable protection: that the cash price should exceed £100 but not £30,000 and that the value of the *credit* should be limited to £15,000. But if a dealer misrepresents the condition of a car, you can rely on S.75 to effectively cancel the contract of purchase and the finance agreement.

The second, familiar form of finance is our old friend, the hire purchase agreement. This is an agreement for the hire of goods generally from a finance company to the retailer who sold them. On the expiry of the hire term you will be given an option to purchase the car, usually at a nominal sum, otherwise title will not pass and ownership of the vehicle remains with the finance company.

A third means of funding is the credit sale. In essence, it is similar to a simple loan as legal title is transferred immediately to the "purchaser". The repayment sum is unsecured. Just as a credit sale is akin to a loan, so conditional sale agreements (the fourth means) resemble hire purchase contracts. Under such an agreement, legal title to the car is postponed until payment of the price or some other condition is fulfilled. For practical purposes, this is therefore the same as hire purchase, but without the notional hiring.

Having entered into one of these agreements to fund the purchase of a much sought after family saloon or sleek sportster, a realisation of impending financial gloom or guilt pangs may take over. There is no blanket right to cancel but where the right does exist it resembles the old cooling-off period under the hire purchase legislation. This right to purchase will not exist if you have signed a finance agreement on trade premises or where there were no oral representations made to you in your presence. The latter scenario will seldom exist, as it is difficult to envisage the sale of a car without the associated patter, but there is generally no right to cancel where the agreement is concluded on the premises of the motor trader or finance company. This may come as quite a shock. Whether a particular finance company or dealer offers the right to cancel is entirely down to its trading conditions. Simply, there is no five or seven day cooling-off period as of right, so check the small print of the proposed agreement very carefully. If in doubt walk away and sleep on what could prove to be a very costly decision.

5.10 BUYING PRIVATELY

Buying privately carries more than its fair share of risk. The basic problem is that the principle of, 'let the buyer beware' applies in large measure. The only enforceable part of the SSGA is that the car must match its description. So, if the seller tells you that the car has a new engine, when in fact it's the original which has covered more than 100,000 miles, you will have a claim on the basis of misrepresentation provided you sustain a loss. But if he'd said nothing, then the risk would be entirely yours.

CASE HISTORY

Mr Collett bought a Jaguar E-type privately. He thought the car was a real peach but it soon turned out to be a lemon: it broke down on the M25 after only 15 miles. Because the seller hadn't made any misrepresentations about the car in any way, Mr Collett had to pick up the £2,000 repair bill on his own. If you are buying privately, always:

⚖ TIPPING THE SCALES OF JUSTICE ⚖

- *Ask the seller as many questions as you can.*
- *Take a witness.*
- *Ask to see all the service documents.*
- *Consider paying for an expert to give it a thorough going over.*
- *Sleep on your decision.*
- *Make a contemporaneous written note of all discussions with the seller.*

Chapter 5 - Databank

AA
Fanum House
Basingstoke, RG21 2EA
0161 485 6000 - Legal Advice
(members only)
0345 500 610 - Vehicle Inspections

DVLA
Swansea, SA99 1TU
01792 782523

HPI Equifax (HPI register checks)
01722 422422

Motor Insurers Bureau (MIB)
152 Silbury Boulevard
Central Milton Keynes
MK9 1NB
01908 240000 - Uninsured and
untraced drivers
01908 671681 (f)

RAC (Legal Services)
0345 300400

Retail Motor Industry Federation
9 North Street
Rugby
CV21 2AB
01788 576465 - Conciliation
service for member garages
01788 547361 (f)

Society of Motor Auctions
9 North Street
Rugby
CV21 2AB
01788 576465 - For complaints
concerning motor auctions

Society of Motor Manufacturers
& Traders
Forbes House
Halk Street
London
SW1X 7QS
0171 235 7000 - New car and
warranty problems
0171 235 7102 (f)

Vehicle Builders and Repairers
Association
Belmont House
Finkle Lane
Gildersome
Leeds
LS27 7TW
0113 2538333 - Accident repairs
0113 2380496 (f)

Automobile Buyers' Services
(ABS)
01625 576441 - Vehicle valuations
and inspections
01625 576438 (f)

Vehicle Valuation Bureau
01225 866333 - Helps to challenge
insurers' write-off values

Alfa Romeo GB
266 Batch Road
Slough
Berkshire
SL1 4HL
01753 511431

BMW (GB) Ltd.
Ellesfield Avenue
Bracknell
Berkshire
RG12 7TA
01344 426565

Citroen UK Ltd.
221 Bath Road
Slough
Berkshire
SL1 4BA
01753 822100

Daihatsu (UK) Ltd.
Poulton Close
Dover
Kent
CT17 0HP
01304 213030

Fiat Auto (UK) Ltd.
266 Batch Road
Slough
Berkshire
SL1 4HL
01753 511431

Ford Motor Company Ltd.
Ford Central Office
Eagle Way
Brentwood
Essex CM13 3BW
0800 231231

Honda UK
Power Road
Chiswick
London
W4 5YT
0181 747 1400

Hyundai (UK) Ltd.
Ryder Street
West Bromwich
Birmingham
B70 0JE
0121 522 2882

Lada Cars
3120 Park Square
Birmingham Business Park
Birmingham
B37 7YN
0121 717 9000

Mazda Cars (UK)
77 Mount Ephraim
Tunbridge Wells
Kent TN4 8BS
01892 511877

Mercedes-Benz (UK) Ltd.
Tongwell
Milton Keynes
Buckinghamshire
MK15 8BA
01908 245000

Mitsubishi Motors
The Colt Car Company Limited
Watermoor
Cirencester
Gloucestershire GL7 1LF
01285 655777

Nissan Motor (GB)
The Rivers Office Park
Denham Way
Maple Cross
Rickmansworth
Hertfordshire WD3 2YS
01923 899999

Peugeot Motor Company
Aldermoor House
Aldermoor Lane
Coventry CV3 1LT
01203 884000

Proton Cars (UK) Ltd.
Proton House
Royal Portbury Dock
Bristol
Avon
BS20 0NH
01275 375475

Renault UK Ltd.
Rivermead Industrial Estate
Westlea
Swindon
Wiltshire SN5 7YA
01793 513888

Rover Cars
P O Box 47
Cowley Body Plant
Oxford OX4 5NL
0800 620820

Saab
Saab House
Globe Park, Marlow
Buckinghamshire SL1 1LY
01628 895603

Seat (UK) Ltd.
Seat House
Gatwick Road
Crawley
West Sussex
RH10 2AX
01293 514141

Skoda UK Ltd.
Garamond Drive
Great Monks Street
Wymbush, Milton Keynes
Buckinghamshire
MK8 8NZ
01908 264000

Subaru (UK) Ltd.
Ryder Street
West Bromwich
Birmingham B70 0JE
0121 522 2000

Suzuki GB Cars Ltd.
46-62 Gatwick Road
Crawley
West Sussex RH10 2XF
01293 518000

Toyota (GB) Ltd.
The Quadrangle
Redhill
Surrey RH1 1PX
01737 768585

Vauxhall Motors
Osbourne Road
Luton
Bedfordshire
LU1 3YT
01582 427200

Volkswagen Audi
VAG (UK) Ltd.
Yeoman's Drive
Blakelands
Milton Keynes
Buckinghamshire
MK14 5AN
01908 601800

Volvo Cars UK Ltd.
Globe Park
Marlow
Buckinghamshire
SL7 1YQ
01628 477977

Chapter 6

The Professionals

"Professionals" very loosely include solicitors, estate agents, surveyors, architects and accountants. We all have to use their services at some time. If you're buying a house you may well need the solicitor, estate agent, surveyor and architect all at once. Ouch! Because of this "professional" tag, consumers of their services tend to expect a fully professional service. This is enforced by the fact that professionals' fees can be very much on the high side. There can also be an air of mystique and snobbery which surrounds professionals. Many people hold them in far too much respect. Remember that after you've instructed someone he is effectively your client. Don't lose sight of this fact. If you feel that your professional is not acting in your best interests, or is charging too much, don't suffer in silence.

There are common rules for complaining about professionals. Although each profession or its governing body may have different procedures to deal with its members, for example a dishonest solicitor could be struck off the Law Society's roll, the following should be considered generally.

6.1 GETTING THE RIGHT PROFESSIONAL

In many respects this is the most critical part of the whole equation. Getting the right man for the job at the outset is far less likely to lead to complaints later on. Membership of a governing body is likely to be compulsory for most professionals so won't be a guarantee of quality. A long list of qualifications is no good either if bedside manner is poor. Opting for the first name in Yellow Pages or your phone book is a bit like putting your hand in a piranha infested pool in the search for hidden treasure. You could strike it lucky, but it all could go horribly wrong.

⚖ TIPPING THE SCALES OF JUSTICE ⚖

- *Go with personal recommendations - ask friends or colleagues about their experiences.*
- *Ask for testimonials or evidence of satisfied customers.*
- *Phone around - telephone manner could often be a good indicator of a professionally run, customer-focused office.*
- *Ask for sales/promotional literature.*
- *Take your time - don't be rushed into making a decision. There are many professionals out there looking for your business.*

CASE HISTORY

Elaine needed an architect to design a new conservatory. Like most people she didn't know anyone personally so looked for names in the Yellow Pages.

She responded to a small, simple ad on the basis that someone who couldn't spend vast sums on advertising, probably charged reasonable fees. What a mistake! The architect did pay her a visit and he did draw up some plans. But the work he proposed was impossible to build yet he charged nearly £2,500 for his services. When Elaine refused to pay he took her to court and got a judgment for £1,400.

6.2 GIVING INSTRUCTIONS

Once you've found what you think to be a reasonable professional for the job, you'll need to give proper instructions. This is critical. Pay a visit to his office. Take with you details of precisely the work that you need to be done. It's no good giving a vague brief or you'll get a vague answer and a big bill. It's a bit like paying a visit to the hairdresser and asking the stylist to, "do as you please." The results can be alarming!

Agree terms of reference. Check the professional's charging structure. Is a one-off fee negotiable? What about guaranteed stage payments? Will the bill cover disbursements or are they extra? Does he add a percentage mark-up to cover, "care and control?" When is payment due - will an up-front non-refundable deposit be required? What about success/contingency fees?

Most professionals will have published business conditions and possibly some kind of Customer Charter. If you require the professional services of someone else, for example a surveyor and an architect, will one oversee the other, or will you be responsible for instructing two separate firms/individuals? Look also for penalty clauses. If you can't go ahead with the arrangement or if say a builder lets you down, will you still be responsible for the professional's fees?

Finally, check that he carries adequate professional indemnity insurance. If he makes an horrendous mistake which could cost you thousands, insurance could be your financial saviour. If you're in any doubt about the security of the professional, ask for a bank reference.

6.3 OVERSEEING THE WORK

There's a very fine dividing line between being a nuisance and leaving the professional alone to get on with their work. But remember, it's your work he's doing and if you're in any doubt or have any questions, pick up the phone!

If you've instructed a good professional, chances are you won't have to chase him for progress. Built into his fee should be provision for interim invoices and reports. But if not, ask for them. If you've instructed a firm, and you're unhappy with the progress of one of its employees/partners, ask for a review from a senior partner. If you've heard nothing for a while don't be embarrassed to phone and chase. The longer he's involved, the larger, potentially, will be his fee. Conversely, if you've agreed a one-off fee, it'll be in his interests to act swiftly so make sure that corners aren't cut. This is particularly true of solicitors doing conveyancing work. The market is very competitive but if all the formalities aren't complied with, you could find a motorway being built in your back garden.

If your work isn't progressing, ask to see the professional's file of papers. Try to work together to mount any unexpected hurdles. Again, if you do your homework early, the professional relationship should run smoothly and amicably. Don't get stroppy or awkward until you have to.

6.4 COMPLAINING

Complaints broadly fall into two categories. Those about charges and those about unprofessional work.

Excessive fees

Again this comes back to doing the groundwork before you instruct a professional. If you've agreed your upper fee limit, then there shouldn't be any nasty surprises when the final bill arrives. It's also advisable to ask for monthly or interim accounts rather than face one hefty bill. If you think that the fees aren't justified, ask for a detailed breakdown of the work involved. If five letters could have got the same result as ten, offer to pay for the five. Were so many site visits really necessary? To a degree you will have to accept his professional word and judgement and it's obviously much easier to challenge clearly excessive fees.

Generally you will be able to secure some movement in the fees claimed. Most professionals accept that pursuing individuals through the courts is an expensive and time consuming process. They are much more likely to agree to a 10-20% reduction.

In some cases, you can complain to the professional's ruling body about excessive fees. The Law Society for example can ask for a solicitor's bill to be taxed in litigation cases or can issue a Certificate of Remuneration in non-contentious matters (see later). Not paying a bill simply because you think it's too high, won't cut any ice. You'll have to justify your position. If you're taken to court and you lose, not only could you have to pay legal costs but a judgment will be registered against your name for six years if you don't settle it within 28 days.

Poor work

Clearly negligent work is often much easier to deal with than minor quibbles. If an architect fails to recommend an RSJ and the roof falls down, his professional insurance should respond swiftly to your claim. Again, make sure that the person you instruct is properly insured. One negligence claim could run into tens of thousands of pounds.

Less serious complaints should be handled carefully. If you act prematurely or complain out of hand, his professional ego can be easily bruised and you could find the work held up further. But wait too long and a minor problem could mushroom into something far more serious. If you've specified a series of deadlines for completion of the work, then the professional is in no position to challenge you for complaining.

If you've made a big mistake and instructed someone clearly not up to the job, don't be in any doubt - sack him! Pay a proportion of his fees to cover that work which was done reasonably, then walk away and find someone else. Allowing such a person to continue will compound the situation and give him the belief that he has your confidence. If you don't catch the problem early, be bullish about complaining. Put your anxieties in writing. Specify where the service is falling down and what has to be done to get it back on track. Threaten to withhold payment if the work doesn't improve. If the situation is serious, send copies of your letters to his senior partner/managing director and his ruling body.

If it's a technical dispute, consider a second or third opinion. Whilst this may cost a few quid, in the long run it'll probably be money well spent.

6.5 REMEDIES

If you can't resolve your complaint amicably by negotiation, there are essentially three options;

1. Litigation.
2. Arbitration.
3. Investigation by a governing body.

1. Litigation

If your claim is for £3,000 or less, consider the small claims procedure of the county court. It's relatively straightforward, cheap and you won't have to pay the other side's legal costs, even if you lose. But if you've had to pay for expensive experts reports, you'll only recover a proportion of their fees. Often the cost of defending small claims proceedings will be your most effective weapon. Taking time to attend court and complete the formalities, coupled with the no-costs rule, can make defending an action uneconomic.

For all other litigation you'll find yourself in the county court proper, or even the High Court. The costs associated with such litigation can be prohibitive so be guided by a solicitor (do your homework in finding the right one!).

2. Arbitration

Many professions run arbitration schemes to resolve complaints. They are usually administered by The Chartered Institute of Arbitrators. It is a private process by which the arbitrator (appointed by the parties to the dispute) will make an award which is final, binding and enforceable in the courts. Generally you won't have to pay towards the arbitrator's fee but you will have to pay a small registration fee. Immediately this gives you a financial advantage over the professional.

3. Governing bodies

For many professionals membership of a professional or governing body is a prerequisite to being able to practice. Withdraw that membership and the professional loses his livelihood - the ultimate sanction. But many governing bodies are regarded as monolithic and keen to protect their own kind. A common criticism of the old Solicitors' Complaints Bureau was that solicitors policed solicitors, often very ineffectively. Whilst such criticism is probably justifiable to a degree, most bodies are today much more aware of their need to serve the public as well as their members. Many subscribe to The Chartered Institute of Arbitrators schemes. Those that don't probably run their own or through another body. In all cases, there's a set complaints procedure to follow. But it's worth noting that in some cases the body concerned cannot get involved. With architects for example, RIBA won't listen to complaints about fees.

Solicitors

Complaints against solicitors are commonplace, particularly in regard to property transactions. Indeed many sole practitioners give the rest of the profession something of a bad name by taking on more work than they can reasonably cope with and then either "losing" clients money or failing to complete formalities on time. Complaints generally fall into three categories - overcharging, poor work and negligence. In respect of overcharging, solicitors cannot provide a detailed estimate as a guarantee of the final bill. But just as if you take your car into a garage and put a financial limit on the work to be carried out, so a solicitor ought to keep you informed as and when these limits are reached. A commonsense approach should be adopted and in any event the bill must be fair and reasonable. If not, then the nature of the complaint will depend upon the type of work which the solicitor did. If it was a litigious matter in which court proceedings had been commenced then the solicitor is required to provide a detailed breakdown of the work done. If this fails to resolve the dispute, the matter is referred to a process called taxation. But if, as is the case with conveyancing, the work is non-contentious you can ask for a Certificate of Remuneration within twenty-eight days of the date of the bill. Under this procedure it is the Law Society which considers the paperwork and decides whether the bill is fair and reasonable or what other sum would be so in all the circumstances. Unlike taxation this service is free and often highly effective.

If the complaint is about poor or slow or unprofessional work, then in the first instance it should be referred to the solicitor's internal complaints handling procedure (if he's part of a firm). Usually the case is given to the senior partner. But of course this process can never be truly impartial and if a solution is not reached, a brief account of the problem should be referred to the Office for the Supervision of Solicitors (Ofsol). If the nature of the complaint is that the solicitor has caused you distress but did not incur any financial loss, then Ofsol provides a system aimed at quickly resolving such problems informally. It can award up to £1,000 in compensation.

Ofsol will also consider much more serious complaints of negligence, which in property cases, could amount to losses of tens of thousands of pounds.

Estate agents

Popular people estate agents. Regrettably this is not the case at all. They have a reputation as having the smoothest of silken tongues, the toughest of hard skin and the deepest of deep pockets. In the popularity stakes they probably rank alongside the tax man and used car dealers. Some of this criticism may be justified. Indeed during the property boom of the 1980's many agents did make a lot of money using their finely tuned and imaginative skills. A broom cupboard could be sold as an aircraft hangar with an appropriate asking price. The late 1980's also saw the proliferation of national chains of estate agents often backed by the major building societies and banks. Being economic with the truth or by employing other sharp practices such as putting in false offers still prevail to a certain extent today.

But in fairness to the profession it would be wrong to tag its members as being any worse than any of the other service professionals. In any event, the property slump and tighter judicial control have meant that consumers are now generally better served and better protected. Obviously the watchword is still very much caution - but this should go without saying when buying such an expensive commodity. Estate agents are governed by the laws of contract and agency, the Estate Agents Act 1979 and the Property Misdescriptions Act 1991.

If you are selling your property, be prepared to negotiate the commission rate payable. It will vary according to the type of agreement you enter into but generally should not exceed 3.5%. Check that there are no fees payable up front and that commission is only due on a completed sale. Are there any hidden extras in respect of photos, advertising or For Sale boards?

National Association of Estate Agents (NAEA)
This Association was established in 1962 with the aims of (amongst others), safeguarding the public against restrictive practices and fraud, misrepresentation and malpractice. Therefore always look for an agent who is a member, as it should show that higher standards have to be attained and that the member is bound by the Association's Rules of Conduct. If you have a complaint against a member, then it should be made in writing and sent to the Association's Executive Committee. If the complaint is upheld the member may be punished by one or more of the following: caution, reprimand, fine, reclassification of membership, suspension or ultimately expulsion.

Ombudsman For Corporate Estate Agents (OCEA)
The OCEA was established in 1990 to provide an independent service for dealing with disputes between Member Agencies and consumers who are either buyers or sellers of residential property in the UK. The scheme covers the majority of major corporate residential estate agency chains in the UK (such as those run by building societies). The Ombudsman will consider complaints of unfair treatment, maladministration and infringement of legal rights. He cannot deal with complaints if;

1. They are not against a Member Agency.
2. They are being dealt with by a court.
3. They relate to a survey dispute.
4. They are for more than £100,000.
5. The complaint is more than 12 months old.
6. If it is sent to the Ombudsman more than 6 months after you receive a settlement offer from the Member Agency concerned.

To complain you must first utilise the Member Agency's internal procedure. If this proves fruitless, formulate your complaint in writing to the Ombudsman. The Ombudsman will then investigate your complaint and ultimately send his decision to both parties. You are not bound to accept his decision but the Member Agency will be bound to pay compensation of up to £100,000 provided you accept the payment on a full and final settlement basis. Otherwise you are free to seek legal redress elsewhere.

Accountants

There are many different types of accountant. Some are little more than book keepers whilst the fully professional chartered accountant is at the other end of the spectrum.

To complain effectively, first raise the matter directly with the accountant. Give evidence of your dissatisfaction and await his response. Many minor complaints can be resolved in this way. The second stage involves writing a formal letter of complaint to the senior partner. The firm's complaints procedure will then take effect and the matter should be considered fully. If the outcome is unfavourable, complaint lies to the governing body, either;

1. The Institute of Chartered Accountants in England and Wales.
2. The Institute of Cost and Management Accountants.
3. The Chartered Institute of Public Finance and Accountancy.
4. The Institute of Chartered Secretaries and Administrators.
5. The Association of Certified Accountants.

Each body has its own disciplinary code to which its members adhere and its own way of dealing with complaints. A preliminary investigation will decide whether to refer the complaint to the full disciplinary committee. Matters of public concern are investigated by the Joint Disciplinary Scheme operated by the three main accountancy bodies.

If you suspect fraud on the part of your accountant in the form of tax evasion or syphoning off your profits, seek professional help from a solicitor. In turn the police could become involved.

Architects

Architects tend to be fairly artistic types so there is scope for instructions to be "misinterpreted". Complaints about fees, delays and failing to act as instructed are the most commonplace. Again, choosing the right professional is crucial. Always complain early about any confusing fees. With building work an architect may well invoice you as the work is completed in stages so clarify any outstanding matters before you part with hard cash.

Complaints about poor conduct should be referred to The Architects' Registration Council of the United Kingdom. But it and The Royal Institute of British Architects (RIBA) have no power to consider complaints about charges or standards. RIBA does publish and police a professional Code of Conduct to which all its members must adhere. Unprofessional conduct could lead to disciplinary action.

Professionals against professionals. One of the biggest hurdles to complaining successfully is getting good independent evidence. It's widely believed that the professions look after themselves and close ranks. Whilst this certainly used to be the case, today most governing bodies keep a register of members who are prepared to take on their "colleagues" in negligence claims.

Chapter 6 - Databank

Royal Institution of Chartered
Surveyors
12 Great George Street
London
SW1 3AD
0171 222 7000
0171 222 9430 (f)

Incorporated Society of Valuers &
Auctioneers
3 Cadogan Gate
London
SW1X 0AS
0171 235 2283
0171 235 4390 (f)

National Association of Estate
Agents
Arbor House
21 Jury Street
Warwick
CV34 4EH
01926 496800
01926 400953 (f)

Office of The Ombudsman for
Corporate Estate Agents
P O Box 1114
Salisbury
Wilts
SP1 1YO
01722 333306
01722 332296 (f)

Law Society of England and Wales
113 Chancery Lane
London
WC2A 1PL
0171 242 1222
01926 822007 (helpline)

Royal Institute of British Architects
66 Portland Place
London
WC1N 4AD
0171 580 5533
0171 255 1541 (f)

Royal Town Planning Institute
26 Portland Place
London
WC1N 4BG
0171 636 9107
0171 323 1582 (f)

The Chartered Institute of
Arbitrators
24 Angel Gate
City Road
London
EC1V 2RS
0171 837 4483

The CIA offers an arbitration
service for, amongst others;

1. Association of British Travel Agents (ABTA)
2. Saga Holidays Ltd.
3. National Caravan Council
4. British Telecommunications plc (BT)
5. Cellnet
6. Racal-Vodaphone Ltd.
7. Mercury Communications Ltd.
8. Orange plc
9. The Cable Television Association
10. The Post Office
11. British Rail
12. National House-Building Council (NHBC)
13. National Association of Estate Agents
14. Glass & Glazing Federation
15. British Association of Removers
16. Law Society (NI)
17. Royal Institution of Chartered Surveyors
18. British Institute of Architectural Technicians
19. Financial Intermediaries, Managers and Brokers Regulatory Association (FIMBRA)
20. Finance Houses Association
21. National Consumer Credit Association
22. Consumer Credit Trade Association
23. Association of Manufacturers of Domestic Electrical Appliances
24. British Photographic Association
25. Mail Order Traders Association
26. British Shops & Stores Association
27. National Association of Funeral Directors

The Association of Certified Accountants
29 Lincoln's Inn Fields
London
WC2A 3EE
0171 242 6855
0171 396 5858 (f)

Chartered Institute of Public Finance and Accountancy
1 Buckingham Place
London
SW1H 6HS
0171 828 7661

The Institute of Chartered Accountants in England and Wales
Chartered Accountants Hall
Moorgate Place
London
EC2P 2BJ
0171 628 7060

The Institute of Cost and Management Accountants
63 Portland Place
London
W1N 4AB
0171 580 6542

The Institute of Chartered Secretaries and Administrators
16 Park Crescent
London
W1N 4AH
0171 580 4741

Architects' Registration Council
of the UK
73 Hallam Street
London
W1N 6EE
0171 580 5861

Office of the Legal Services
Ombudsman
22 Oxford Court
Oxford Street
Manchester
M2 3WQ
0161 236 9532
0161 236 2657

Office for the Supervision of
Solicitors
Victoria Court
8 Dormer Place
Leamington Spa
Warwickshire
CV32 5AE
01926 820082
01926 431435

Chapter 7

Health

As the nation ages and standards of medicine improve, we become bigger consumers of health services. This chapter is not heavily concerned with the services provided by the NHS. We don't after all pay for them in the same way as say a chiropractor or a herbalist. Alternative and complementary medicine are big business. Some have the blessing and support of "traditional" medicine, some clearly don't. It is doubtful whether some of the treatments currently available are truly medicinal at all. The great risk for consumers of these services is that they're unregulated. How safe is it to take Chinese herbs? What if the treatment goes horribly wrong? Is there a governing body or an approved register of Chinese homeopaths?

It is likely that regulation of these quasi-medicinal branches of the health service will be introduced in due course. But until then, it *is* worth shopping around and checking on the protection that is currently available.

7.1 GP's

If you live in the UK you have the right to be registered with a General Practitioner (GP). When you move to a new area, chances are that you won't have any knowledge of the GP's so it maybe a question of pot luck. Your local Family Health Services Authority (FHSA, details in the 'phone book) will provide a list of GP's.

Once you've been accepted into the practice you're entitled to the following:

- Details of the facilities offered by the practice.
- A mini health check-up on first registration.
- Details of the 24 hour emergency service.
- A consultation with a GP at any time during surgery hours (unless an appointment system is in operation).
- Be told about your illness fully and truthfully.
- Have access to your medical records (unless the doctor considers this to be harmful to you).
- A clear explanation of any treatment proposed.
- Refuse treatment at any time.
- Confidentiality from your GP. Doctors aren't allowed to pass on information about you without your consent unless it's to other people involved in your treatment or to close relatives. The law can order doctors to divulge certain information. For example, if required by a court or you're suspected of being a drug addict.

If you've a complaint about your GP, to whom you complain will depend upon the nature of the complaint. The General Medical Council (GMC) is the self-governing body for GP's. It exists primarily to protect the public interest. It can take action;

- When a GP has been convicted of a criminal offence.
- When there is an allegation of serious professional misconduct. This could include sexual impropriety, heavy drinking etc.
- When your GP is incapable of treating you because of his own mental/physical illness.

The GMC has a wide range of sanctions it can impose if your complaint is upheld, the most serious of which involves striking off the register.

Lesser complaints should be made in writing to your FHSA within 13 weeks of the incident. If upheld, the GP may well be given a formal warning.

If you think you've been treated negligently and your illness has worsened or you've suffered in some other way, your claim will have to be proven in the courts. You'll need the help of a solicitor, so shop wisely for the best professional (Chapter 6).

7.2 OPTICIANS
The General Optical Council (GOC) is the statutory body responsible for the registration of opticians and for matters relating to their education and discipline. It has no power to intervene in complaints about contact lenses or spectacles. But it is responsible for all matters relating to misconduct or malpractice.

CASE HISTORY
Arthur wanted some new specs. He visited his local branch of "Eyes R Us." During the sight test, the optician told Arthur that he was gay and started to stroke his hair. He asked Arthur out to a local gay bar and suggested that they could, "have a great time together." Arthur immediately reported this gross misconduct to the GOC. Its Disciplinary Committee investigated, set up a hearing and eventually struck the optician off the register thereby preventing him from practising ever again. * Note - The GOC cannot award compensation to consumers.

NHS treatment from an optician can also be referred to the FHSA. It has the same powers as if the complaint is against a GP.

If the complaint relates to the standard or cost of the service, spectacles or contact lenses try initially to resolve it with the optician concerned. The most common disputes relate to charges. The marketplace is very competitive and most consumers buy from one of the high street multiples. There are many good deals available such as free frames or sunglasses. But check the conditions of such offers very carefully.

⚖ *TIPPING THE SCALES OF JUSTICE* ⚖

1. *Good deals on glasses often hide expensive sight tests.*
2. *Check to see exactly what's included - with spectacles, you'll need to know the price for a test, the frames and the lenses. Extras can soon mount up for tints and lens coatings. Contact lenses, particularly disposable ones, are big business. If you're buying the odd pair, check the replacement insurance cover. If it's disposables you're after, check what the monthly charge covers. Is there a penalty if you change your mind or find them to be unsuitable?*

If you can't resolve the dispute amicably, refer it to The Optical Consumer Complaints Service. It can investigate and award compensation where complaints are upheld.

7.3 DENTISTS

For obvious reasons, dentists aren't particularly popular people. Many practices have now opted out of NHS work or only keep a few NHS patients on their books. Dental treatment is expensive so many consumers take out private schemes with the likes of BUPA or Denplan. The premium you pay will be rated according to your oral health. A neglected set of molars could lead to an expensive policy. Free NHS dental cover is only available to the following:

1. Those under 18.
2. Those under 19 if still in full-time education.
3. Pregnant women or those who've had a baby in the past 12 months.
4. Those on income support or family credit (or their partners).
5. Those in possession of an NHS certificate.

So if you're a private patient, again make sure you know what you're paying for. The mere fact that the dentist is a health professional doesn't lessen your consumer rights in anyway. When you buy a three piece suite you're given the opportunity to examine it properly and you'll be told all the costs. With a dentist it's a bit difficult to challenge what he's doing with a mouthful of drill. And to a degree, if the work he does isn't in your opinion up to scratch, you'll probably need a second opinion to confirm your worst fears. Again, many complaints are about charges. The dentist should provide you with a detailed estimate of the likely costs. Always ask for one and specify an upper limit on what you can afford. If he goes beyond that don't pay.

Complaints about NHS treatment from dentists are investigated by the FHSA. In cases involving serious professional misconduct, the allegation is considered by the General Dental Council. The Council is under a duty to maintain a register of dentists in which the public can have confidence. It has no power to punish offenders directly. All it can do is erase or suspend from the register any dentist which it considers unfit to practice.

7.4 VETS
As a pet-loving nation, visits to the vet are becoming more commonplace. And as there's no NHS for animals, it can be a very expensive exercise. Insurance schemes help but complaints still arise.

The governing body is The Royal College of Veterinary Surgeons. It has a fairly limited role in complaint investigation and will only intervene in areas relating to an allegation of professional misconduct. It is important to distinguish this from questions about professional competence over which the RCVS has no authority. So if you think that the vet has made a wrong diagnosis, or prescribed damaging drugs or otherwise been negligent, you'll have to pursue a legal claim. This will involve a solicitor and another vet who's prepared to question the judgement of the first.

But many minor complaints can be readily resolved by having an informed word with the vet concerned. A misunderstanding about the treatment proposed can arise during times of stress. So don't be shy about seeking a full explanation. If the vet's conduct is unprofessional, for example, he makes improper advances, or speaks out of turn or has a drink/drugs problem, you must complain in writing to the RCVS.

7.5 OSTEOPATHS
There are in excess of 2,000 osteopaths working in the UK. Their worth has long been recognised and the 1993 Osteopaths Act gave the profession statutory regulation - the first of the complementary health practitioners. This is good news because a soon to be established General Osteopathic Council will replace the existing unregulated voluntary bodies. It will only allow those practitioners who can satisfy its requirements to be admitted to

the register and to use the term "osteopath". The Council will also be responsible for policing its members and for investigating complaints.

Currently anyone can set up as an osteopath so you take a chance if they're not properly qualified and a member of one of the voluntary bodies. Always try to go with a personal recommendation and not the first name in the phone book. Check fee scales and, importantly, the level of liability cover. If your back is put literally out of joint, suing an osteopath personally could be a long and ultimately fruitless exercise.

7.6 COMPLEMENTARY PRACTITIONERS

The British Register of Complementary Practitioners (BRCP) provides consumers with a choice of "qualified" practitioners. These alternative health service providers are not, generally, governed by legislation and to a degree still operate in the grey void between traditional medicine and quackery. Being on the Register is no guarantee of quality or that legally enforceable minimum standards of education/training have been attained. And if all goes horribly wrong there's no FHSA or GMC to complain to. But BRCP members do carry public liability, professional indemnity and, where necessary, product liability insurance, so do try to find a registered practitioner. The National Register has various divisions covering most branches of complementary medicine. The following are included;

- **Aromatherapy**
- **Chromatherapy**
- **Energy medicine**
- **Homeopathy**
- **Indian medicine**
- **Massage**
- **Osteopathy**

- **Remedial massage**
- **Chinese medicine**
- **Hypnotherapy**
- **Japanese medicine**
- **Nutrition**
- **Reflexology**

With all of these practitioners, choosing the right one is of course critical. If you feel in any way unhappy, terminate the consultation. Refer to your GP for his opinion. It's not advisable to sign up for a long series of treatments especially if you're asked to pay up-front. Pay as you go along. This way any losses will be kept to a minimum.

7.7 HOMEOPATHS

Homeopaths may be registered with the BRCP. There is also The Society of Homeopaths Limited. Again homeopaths are not governed by statute but the Society has a formal complaints investigation procedure.

But of course your neighbour who dabbles in homeopathic remedies is unlikely to be a member of the Society. If you suffer a reaction you'd be left with a civil action claiming damages. But you'd have to prove negligence - probably poor advice or a poor assessment of your condition.

The best advice is treat complementary medicine with caution. It doesn't claim to offer answers to all physical and mental problems and, at present the profession is fragmented, largely unregulated and peppered with cowboys.

Chapter 7 - Databank

General Medical Council (GMC)
44 Hallam Street
London
W1N 6AE
0171 580 7642
0171 915 3641 (f)

Health Service Ombudsman
Church House
Great Smith Street
London, SW1P 3BW
0171 276 3035
0171 276 2104 - complaints about the NHS

The United Kingdom Central Council for Nursing (UKCC)
23 Portland Place
London, W1 3AF
0171 637 7181 - complaints about nurses, midwives or health visitors

General Optical Council
41 Harley Street
London
W1N 2DJ
0171 580 3898
0171 436 3525 (f)

The Optical Consumer Complaints Service
P O Box 4685
London SE1 8YH
0171 261 1017

General Dental Council
37 Wimpole Street
London
W1M 8DQ
0171 486 2171
0171 224 3294 (f)

British Complementary Medicine Association
39 Prestbury Road
Cheltenham
Gloucestershire
GL52 2PT
01242 226770
01242 267708 (f)

The Osteopathic Information Service
P O Box 2074
Reading
Berkshire
RG1 4YR

Institute for Complementary
Medicine/British Register of
Complementary Practitioners
P O Box 194
London
SE16 1QZ

General Council & Register of
Osteopaths
56 London Street
Reading
Berkshire
RG1 4SQ
0118 9576585

The College of Osteopaths
Practitioners Association
13 Furzehill Road
Borehamwood
Hertfordshire
WD6 2DG
0181 905 1937

The Guild of Osteopaths
497 Bury New Road
Prestwich
Manchester
M25 5AD
0161 798 6352

Natural Therapeutic and
Osteopathic Society and Register
63 Collingwood Road
Witham
Essex
CM8 2EE
01376 512188

British and European Osteopathic
Association
262a Caledonian Road
London
N1 0NG
0171 837 5045

The Royal College of Veterinary
Surgeons
Belgravia House
62-64 Horseferry Road
London
SW1P 2AF
0171 222 2001
0171 222 2004

Patients Charter
Freepost
London
SE99 7XU

British Chiropractic Association
29 Whitley Street
Reading
RG2 0EG
01734 757557
01734 757257 (f)

National Institute of Medical
Herbalists
56 Longbrook Street
Exeter
EX4 6AH
01392 426022
01392 498963 (f)

Chapter 8

Finance And Insurance Services

Banks, building societies and insurance companies are often considered the consumer's enemy - a necessary evil. Seldom do we hear of such institutions making anything other than large profits at the expense of consumers. And even when insurers are hit by particularly bad perils such as earthquakes or floods, the consumer takes the hit the following year with an increased premium.

To a degree the banks and insurance companies really do have the consumer over a barrel. The David and Goliath scenario often arises and it would be unusual to spend a lifetime with a bank without a complaint of some description, however minor. In a time of downsizing, rationalisation and mergers, many high street presences have gone. Bums on seats have been replaced with computers and customer service has suffered. But effective complaining will bring results.

8.1 BANKS AND BUILDING SOCIETIES

When you first open an account you're effectively entering into a contract with the institution concerned. You'll be bound by its terms and conditions so shop around and read all the literature carefully. If you're unsure of a particular condition, ask for it to be clarified. You should check how the bank/building society charges. What about a free overdraft? Are the fees charged on a sliding scale? How much will the bank charge for writing a letter to tell you off?

CASE HISTORY

Keith had been in substantial funds with his bank for 17 years. When he moved house he accidentally ran his current account into a £26 unauthorised overdraft. The bank wrote a stroppy letter advising Keith that he'd been charged £25. Naturally he was incensed and wrote a strong letter of complaint. His bank offered an immediate apology and reimbursed the £25 penalty charge.

Keith's is a good example of a bank failing to look at a customer's individual circumstances and a computer reacting automatically to an unauthorised transaction.

Complaints about banks and building societies should initially be made to the branch manager in writing. If you suspect a problem with your account or if you've been charged unreasonably, voice your concerns immediately. Always check your statements carefully otherwise you could be compounding the problem. The bank could also get awkward if a problem is apparent or ought to have been apparent by looking at a statement. Get as much evidence of your complaint as possible. If the branch manager can't help or you don't accept his proposal, the complaint will then be referred to his regional manager.

In turn the facts will be considered afresh. If there is clearly no hope of reaching a settlement, the institution concerned must issue a letter of deadlock. Only at that stage can the matter be referred to either The Office of The Banking Ombudsman or The Office of The Building Societies Ombudsman. Both receive broadly the same number of complaints annually and can make binding awards of up to £100,000. They are appointed by, and are responsible to, an independent Council. For the Banking Ombudsman most complaints relate to lending, charges and interest. The Building Societies Ombudsman tends to receive most complaints about mortgages. Remember of course that several of the former principal building societies now have full bank status. Their terms of reference permit the Ombudsman to deal with all types of banking/building society business transacted through the branch network or by telephone. They cannot investigate complaints about general policies or commercial decisions for making loans unless there has been maladministration.

There is also The Code of Good Banking Practice which applies to both banks and building societies. The Code is voluntary but certainly helps consumers by requiring banks to, "*act fairly and reasonably in all their dealings with their customers.*" The Ombudsman will consider whether the institute complained of has acted within the spirit of the Code.

Cash machines (ATM's)

A special mention for the "hole in the wall" cash machine. Under the original code, a customer's liability for unauthorised ATM withdrawals was capped at £50. This figure remains unless the customer has been guilty of fraud or gross negligence. It is a clear contractual requirement and a condition of issue of an ATM card, to keep it separate from the PIN. Gross negligence could be a failure to keep the two separate or for example writing the PIN on the back of the card. In such a case your liability could be limited to the amount in your account.

8.2 INSURANCE COMPANIES

Claiming against an insurance policy can be like a living hell. Claimants tend to fall into two categories - those who feel they must claim on an annual basis to get some value for money from the annual premium, and those who genuinely claim only when the need arises. In some cases this may be never even though thousands of pounds may have been committed to insurance premiums. Of course we have all heard of horrendous stories from friends and family who have had problems claiming. But then exceptional cases are always more newsworthy than those which proceed without a problem. Human nature. The insurance industry as a whole has a poor reputation when it comes to claims, but well supported, evidenced and reasonable submissions ought to pass through the insurers hands relatively speedily. Slow claims are just as often the fault of the claimant if you have only provided part of the information requested or generally been unhelpful. A failure to understand policy limitations can also be a major stumbling block.

Claiming is very much a question of commonsense and *generally* insurers will do what they can to assist. The market for household insurance is now very competitive so attaining the market edge in terms of customer service may be crucial to the insurance company concerned. Much business is now placed with the direct market - you simply pick up a telephone, give your details and cover is effected immediately. In such cases it is usual to pay by credit card or to agree to put a cheque in the post immediately. At this point, the contract of insurance is valid. Problems do occur with the automated quotation systems and it may be that your insurer subsequently says that it made a mistake and you owe some more. Provided you gave all the correct information and acted with utmost good faith at the time, the cost of the mistake should be borne by the insurance company. However, it may only offer a provisional quote on the telephone subject to a consideration of the proposal form. In such cases you may be asked to pay an additional sum. Many insurers offer twenty-four hour helplines giving easy access to a range of tradesmen and professionals. At a time of crisis, expert advice may be critical in ensuring that losses are mitigated and that the claims process gets off on the correct footing.

With all types of insurance claim, you must check to see whether your policy specifies a time limit for either notifying of a potential claim or submitting the correct claim form. If it is a burglary/theft/criminal damage claim, you will need a police report or crime reference number. If you require urgent building work, you may have to call out a twenty-four hour contractor to effect emergency repairs. Thereafter be guided by your insurer.

In terms of complaint there are several options open to you. Always act reasonably and try not to consider your grievance too subjectively. *Never* fight solely on a point of principle - you *will* fail. You should collate as much evidence in support as possible and, if necessary, be prepared to seek an independent expert's report, the cost of which may be added to your claim if successful. If you have arranged your business through a broker, he may be invaluable in assessing the merits of your complaint objectively. He will also have experience of insurance companies generally and should be able to direct you along the right path. If you've bought directly, then try to deal with the same individual every time you telephone or correspond. Always formulate and follow up your complaint in writing, quoting the correct reference. Keep copies of all correspondence. Each insurance company will have its own complaints procedure which you should follow. If this fails, then effectively you have four options:

1. Sue for damages in the civil courts. Costly, complex, very lengthy and in all but the most serious cases, probably too risky.
2. Complain to the Insurance Ombudsman Bureau.
3. If not a member of the IOB scheme you could contact the Personal Insurance Arbitration Scheme (PIAS) which is operated by the Association of British Insurers. Here an independent arbitrator will be appointed to consider the complaint. It can be quite an effective remedy, but has two principal drawbacks: firstly, both parties must consent to the procedure and secondly, once you have agreed to arbitration, you lose your right to sue in the civil courts.
4. Back down gracefully!

The Ombudsman is the most favoured scheme and deserves more attention. In essence the IOB was founded in 1981 by a group of major insurance companies to provide an independent and impartial method of resolving complaints. There are now over three hundred and fifty members of the IOB scheme. To be considered by the IOB your complaint must:

1. Have first been put to the insurance company concerned's own complaints procedure.
2. Be passed to the IOB within six months of the stalemate between you and the insurer.
3. Relate to a UK, Isle of Man or Channel Islands claim.
4. Relate to a claim on the administration or marketing of your policy.

It is also important to note that the IOB cannot intervene if the complaint is already being dealt with through the courts, or is in respect of a decision relating to cover. The IOB is a very busy office and in 1996 responded to 16,000 written enquiries and 50,000 telephone enquiries providing advice and assistance on the pursuit of complaints. If your complaint falls within the IOB's remit, it will be handled by a consideration of all the papers and a liaison between the parties concerned. Experts may be consulted. Eventually (in 1996 the average case took 135 days to process) the Ombudsman will make a decision which will be sent in writing to you and the other party. The Ombudsman can award up to £100,000 in your favour, but his decision is not binding until accepted. If you reject the decision you are free to pursue other remedies. There is no cost to you and the insurance company is bound by the award. Also in 1996, the highest award was £167,600 and the lowest £3! The most common complaints to the IOB by far in terms of general insurance relate to motor and household disputes.

It is clear that if your insurer is a member of the IOB scheme, the procedure it offers for dealing with complaints can be of real value, particularly as you are not bound to accept any decision.

8.3 INSURANCE BROKERS/INTERMEDIARIES

Most people who sell insurance are not brokers in the true legal sense. Only those registered with the Insurance Brokers' Registration Council can legally call themselves a broker. The IBRC issues a Code of Conduct which requires brokers to put clients' interests first, avoid using misleading language and to observe the utmost integrity and good faith. It also has a disciplinary committee to investigate complaints of unprofessional conduct.

There are surprisingly few registered brokers. Practically anyone can carry on the business of a broker without being registered. Such intermediaries may trade as insurance consultants or advisors or even as limited companies. But anyone whose business involves investment must be authorised by the Financial Services Act. The Act offers protection in the event of a failure to comply with the rules of investment.

When placing pure insurance with non-registered brokers you do take something of a risk. Always look for a company which belongs to the Association of British Insurers (ABI). Not only does the ABI issue a binding Code of Practice but requires its members to carry professional negligence insurance.

⚖ TIPPING THE SCALES OF JUSTICE ⚖

1. *If you can't find a registered broker, look for an intermediary who's an ABI member.*
2. *Always be specific with your instructions - many intermediaries are good salesman and you could end up spending more than necessary.*

Complaints about intermediaries often relate to the insurer itself refusing to accept a claim. One of the fundamental principles of the insurance contract is that the insured must act with utmost good faith and disclose all material information to assess the risk. If the intermediary gave false or misleading information just to get you covered, you won't have a gripe against the actual insurer. But you'll almost certainly be in a position to sue the intermediary for your losses.

8.4 FINANCIAL ADVISORS

Financial advisors have been criticised in the past for giving very little advice but doing a lot of hard selling. Getting independent financial advice is still difficult. If you're dealing with a tied agent, he can only advise on and sell his company's products, such as Allied Dunbar. So-called Independent Financial Advisors (IFA's) are supposed to act as a broker and offer independent, impartial advice on a whole range of potentially suitable products and services. They're also supposed to tell you exactly how much commission they earn from each policy sold. This should allow you to make an informed decision. In practice of course there is still ample scope for persuasive selling.

The overall responsibility for the regulation of financial services is with the Securities and Investments Board (SIB). In turn it oversees the work of several self-regulatory organisations such as FIMBRA, Lautro and IMRO (the latter two being superseded by the Personal Investment Authority, PIA). Therefore always seek out an authorised advisor. Although self-regulating, the powers of these bodies are far reaching and provide protection to personal investors. Moreover, unless authorised, certain investment activities are illegal and could land the advisor in a lot of hot water (or gaol!) The PIA is now the main body which regulates firms that sell investments to the public. It will investigate complaints relating to life assurance, unit trusts, PEPS, personal pensions, share dealing, investment trust savings schemes and guaranteed income bonds (amongst others). Here are some requirements of financial advisors involved with investment business;

- You must be told how much commission they'll get.
- Your money must be paid into a special client account.
- They must offer the best advice for you.
- Their advertisements must be positively truthful and not misleading.

It's worth pointing out that the provision of mortgages is not regulated by the Financial Services Act and that general insurance such as house contents and pure savings schemes are not governed by SIB rules.

Chapter 8 - Databank

Insurance Ombudsman Bureau
135 Park Street
London SE1 9EA
0171 928 7600

Personal Insurance Arbitration
Service
24 Angel Gate, City Road
London EC1V 2RS
0171 837 4483

British Insurance and Investment
Brokers Association
BIIBA House
14 Bevis Marks
London EC3A 7NT
0171 623 9043

The Office of the Banking
Ombudsman
70 Gray's Inn Road
London WC1X 8NB
0171 404 9944
0171 405 5052 (f)

The Office of the Building
Societies Ombudsman
Grosvenor Gardens House
35-37 Grosvenor Gardens
London SW1X 7AW
0171 931 0044
0171 931 8485 (f)

Insurance Brokers' Registration
Council
15 St. Helen's Place
London EC3A 6DS
0171 588 4387

Securities and Investments Board
Gavrelle House
2-14 Bunhill Row
London EC1Y 8RA
0171 638 1240
0171 382 5900 (f)

Association of British Insurers
51 Gresham Street
London
EC2V 7HQ
0171 600 3333

Personal Investment
Authority Ltd.
Consumer Helpdesk
1 Canada Square
Canary Wharf
London E14 5AZ
0171 538 8860 - the main body
which regulates firms that sell
investments to the public. Offers
an effective complaints procedure

Finance and Leasing Association
18 Upper Grosvenor Street
London W1X 9PB
0171 491 2783
0171 629 0396 - can help with
credit problems

CCN Systems Ltd.
Consumer Affairs Department
P O Box 40
Nottingham
NG7 2SS
0115 9410888 - credit reference
agency

CDMS
CCA Department
Dove Mill
Dean Church Lane
Bolton
Lancashire
BL3 4ET
A credit reference agency

Equifax Europe Ltd.
CCA Department
Regency House
38 Whitworth Street
Manchester
M60 1QH
0161 236 8511
A credit reference agency

Chapter 9

Media And Communications

Not so long ago a computer capable of carrying out even the most basic of functions would have taken up an entire room. Today a laptop PC can link you to every corner of the globe in a few seconds from the comfort of your armchair. And remember the telephone-free idyll? Now, with a GSM phone you could be fishing for salmon on a Scottish river and conducting business with your factory in Australia. Skyfones, Satphones, digital phones, Global Positioning Systems lead the technological race to make sure that we're never alone and out of touch.

The Internet and the Information Superhighway delivered to our living rooms by cable TV providers supply an almost unbelievable menu of information, entertainment, services and of course, shopping opportunities. But in regulatory terms we're all a bit in the dark - is it safe to buy goods using the Internet? What about children tapping into explicit sex scenes whilst running up huge phone bills?

9.1 TELEPHONES

British Telecom (BT) has lost its monopoly. Whilst other telephone service providers have not flooded the market as anticipated, nevertheless, there is now room for healthy competition. Once you sign up a supply contract with BT (or Mercury or one of the cable suppliers), the usual rules of contract law apply. But the supplier's principal advantage over its subscribers is that your telephone can be disconnected if the bill is not paid. Unlike consumer credit agreements there is no period of grace to pay the bill. Technically it is payable on demand. A reminder and final notice will be sent, but questions answered later!

Complaining

In terms of an excessive bill, to avoid being disconnected, it is probably advisable to pay at least the part with which you agree. You should then, ideally in writing, complain to the supplier concerned. It will check the line, your equipment and any other factors which could have given rise to erroneous readings. Most subscribers are now on digital exchanges which produce itemised bills (for calls of more than a certain length). These should go some way to alleviating any problems about billing. However, if you reach deadlock, then you really only have two options;

1. Sue using the small claims procedure of the county court.
2. Involve The Office of Telecommunications (Oftel).

Whilst everyone is entitled to their day in court, for most disputes, the county court is probably not the most suitable forum. It can be a quite cumbersome and time-consuming process. It should therefore be seen as something of a last resort or to be used in the more complex cases.

9.2 MOBILE TELEPHONES

Mobile phones are very popular - around 6 million Britons own one. But buying one can be daunting and making the wrong choice could cost you dear.

Whilst free or very cheap phones look tempting, there are usually hidden costs. Remember that the hardware itself is expensive to produce so the suppliers have to recoup their costs, usually in one of three ways (or a combination):

1. Expensive line rental charges.
2. Expensive call costs.
3. Fixing the minimum term of the agreement.

Generally, the cheaper the phone, the more expensive it will be to run. A mobile phone is likely to cost at least £180 - £200 to run every year - and that's before call costs are added.

Getting advice on the right phone, the right network and the right tariff is difficult. There are six networks - Cellnet analogue or digital, Vodafone analogue or digital, One2One and Orange. Cellnet and Vodafone have the most extensive coverage both in the UK and overseas. With both of these networks you'll join through a third party called a service provider (such as Securicor, Martin Dawes etc.). In the cases of Orange and One2One you'll deal direct.

Things to look for when shopping around:

- Check for special offers - is the connection fee waived?
- How much is the monthly line rental inclusive of VAT?
- How widespread is the coverage?
- How are calls charged? Digital phones may be more expensive but charge by the second.
- Will you need to use your phone abroad?
- How much more expensive are peak rate calls?
- Will you be using the phone primarily for incoming calls or making a lot yourself? (if so, consider an all-inclusive Talk Plan like those offered by Orange).
- Can you break the contract early without penalty?

- Which extra features do you really need and how much extra will they cost? For example, the cost of retrieving a message from your personal mailbox could vary massively between networks.
- What about battery life - is a long standby or talk time a requirement?
- Insurance and warranties - what if you break or lose the phone? If not offered as part of the package it's probably worth paying an additional premium for peace of mind.
- What about pre-payment schemes? After the connection fee and the pre-payment, there are no additional charges.

⚖ TIPPING THE SCALES OF JUSTICE ⚖

- *Do your homework - work out what the phone will cost to run including all the hidden extras.*
- *Check the small print of the contract before signing.*

Contracts

A mobile phone agreement is governed by the usual contract law principles. Provided the terms and conditions are reasonable, you'll be bound by them. This means that if you don't pay on time, you'll be disconnected. You could be sued for the outstanding sum. You'll almost certainly be blacklisted. Most agreements are for a minimum of 12 months. Make sure that you can afford to run the phone for this period. If you try to back out early, the service provider/network will pursue you for the outstanding months' line rental.

Cloning

Older, analogue phones can be cloned relatively easily. It goes something like this - when a mobile phone makes a call it sends out two crucial pieces of information - your number and the identity of the piece of equipment being used. The analogue network (Cellnet, Vodafone) checks that the two numbers tally before allowing the call to continue. But hackers using a scanner can eavesdrop this information and download it into a personal computer and duplicate the identity of the original call. Because it usually takes a month for these calls to find their way to the legitimate customer's bill, users who've bought the cloned number can run up hundreds of pounds worth of calls before the problem is detected and the number withdrawn.

Whilst the analogue networks will eventually be withdrawn, fraud on this scale is estimated to cost the industry around £5m every year. If it's your number which is cloned, the good news is that you won't be responsible for the phantom calls - provided you report an anomaly with the bill immediately. Digital phones are undoubtedly more secure but any calls registered on the bill of which you have no knowledge should again be reported. The longer a problem persists, the weaker your position will become.

Complaining

If you have a problem with the network or service provider which you cannot resolve yourself, get in touch with the industry regulator, Oftel. Detail your complaint in writing with as much supporting evidence as possible. Explain what it is you are looking for - an apology or compensation.

9.3 THE INTERNET

Using the Internet poses a whole new set of worries. The main problem is that because of its truly international nature, regulation and control is almost impossible.

Essentially, anyone with a PC, telephone line and modem can gain access to the Internet (millions of pages of electronic information) and surf away. The cost can be relatively small provided off peak telephone services are utilised and you don't spend hours tapping away. You'll need some extra software to get onto the Net or you could go through an on-line service provider such as AOL or Compuserve (they provide access to the World Wide Web as well as offering their own range of services). For a fixed monthly fee of perhaps £10 you may get free e-mail and a certain number of free minutes browsing every month. Premium services cost more and there's always the phone bill to consider on top.

Once you've logged on, the opportunities for enjoyment, information and even shopping stretch as far as your imagination. And there's the problem. There is precious little control over the countless pages of obscene pornography and other junk which is dumped on to the web everyday.

Although videos are censored and broadcasters are regulated heavily, especially until the watershed, your children could find themselves unwittingly e-mailing a child pornographer at breakfast time. So unless (or until) proper controls are introduced, parental control must be carefully exercised.

Shopping on the Internet, although in its relative infancy is likely to become big business very soon. There is naturally concern that giving credit card details could lead to widespread fraud. This is no more likely than giving the details over the phone to say a ticket agency, tour operator or restaurant. The same rules apply - deal with reputable retailers and you should be safe. In any event Consumer Credit Act protection may be available (see Chapter 1).

Chapter 10

Complaint Letters

```
┌─────────────────────────────────────────────────────────┐
│              TEN GOLDEN RULES FOR COMPLAINING             │
│                                                           │
│              1.  Register your complaint early.           │
│          2.  Always follow up a complaint in writing.     │
│        3.  Get as much supporting evidence as possible.   │
│     4.  Don't complain without knowing what you want to   │
│            happen - an apology, a replacement or cash.    │
│              5.  Try to deal with the same person.        │
│   6.  Don't complain solely on a point of principle - and │
│                        expect to win.                     │
│  7.  Think laterally - don't get bogged down with one     │
│       remedy - there are usually several ways to resolve  │
│                         a problem.                        │
│                8.  Keep calm and stay polite.             │
│                    9.  Don't get greedy.                  │
│                    10. Be reasonable.                     │
└─────────────────────────────────────────────────────────┘
```

The first letter of complaint is often crucial. If at all possible, always have it typed. Keep it short and simple - detail the nature of the complaint, what you are seeking by way of redress and when you expect to get it. Whilst supporting evidence should be alluded to, it's not worth making too great a play of it early on.

Chapter 1 - A Shopper's Paradise

27 Dissatisfaction Villas
Gripe Street
Moan City
TX9 3XX

Dear Sir

Arizona Three Piece Suite - £399

Doubtless your records will confirm that I purchased the above furniture from your premises on June 17th. Within a week it became apparent that the goods are not of satisfactory quality as required to be by Section 14 of The Sale and Supply of Goods Act 1994. In particular, the fabric is ripped and dirty, the cushions don't match and one of the springs has failed already. You are therefore in breach of contract entitling me to seek a full refund of the purchase price.

I expect to receive your cheque in the sum of £399 within the next fourteen days and your proposals to remove the furniture from my home. Whilst litigation is to be avoided, I fully intend to pursue the matter through the courts should you fail to comply with your legal obligations.

I look forward to hearing from you.

Yours faithfully

Chapter 2 - Getting Good Service

27 Dissatisfaction Villas
Gripe Street
Moan City
TX9 3XX

Dear Sir

Conservatory Construction

I am in receipt of your invoice dated 8th July. The amount you claim is considerably higher than your firm's original quotation prepared in May which clearly stipulated a fixed price for the work. I understand that because it was a formal fixed quotation, you are bound by it and any additional costs due to unforeseen circumstances should be borne by you.

I therefore enclose a cheque for the amount originally agreed in full and final settlement. I hope that this concludes the matter satisfactorily.

Yours faithfully

27 Dissatisfaction Villas
Gripe Street
Moan City
TX9 3XX

Dear Madam

Damage to Curtains

You will recall that I attended your premises yesterday to complain about the above silk curtains. To reiterate, the colour has faded to an unacceptable level and the curtains have now shrunk to such a degree that they don't fit the windows. You have denied any responsibility. I claim that you were negligent and will have recourse to the courts as you continue to deny responsibility. I'm also referring this complaint to the Textile Services Association.

Yours faithfully

Chapter 3 - Hotels And Restaurants

27 Dissatisfaction Villas
Gripe Street
Moan City
TX9 3XX

Dear Sir

Birthday Dinner - August 17th

On the above date, you entertained my party. It was a special occasion which had been made plain to you at the time of booking. The meal was a disaster. I was so embarrassed. Because I didn't wish to disappoint my guests, I paid the bill in full at the time under protest and reserved my right to claim compensation subsequently. I am now doing this and expect full recompense within the next seven days. If you're not prepared to comply then regrettably I will have no alternative but to issue proceedings using the small claims procedure of the county court.

I look forward to hearing from you by return.

Yours faithfully

Chapter 4 - Holidays From Hell

27 Dissatisfaction Villas
Gripe Street
Moan City
TX9 3XX

Dear Sir/Madam

Hotel Calypso - Barbados
Booking Ref: 89/7627

We have just returned from our honeymoon in Barbados. It was an absolute disaster.

Please find attached a copy of my completed Complaint Form which I submitted to your rep on location. It details in full the nature of my complaint but in essence, the air conditioning never worked, the bedroom was cockroach infested, there were no sun loungers, the pool was out of commission for seven of the fourteen days and the food was disgusting.

My new wife and I had a thoroughly miserable honeymoon and were forced to eat out for much of the time and to visit an adjoining hotel which charged us to use their loungers and pool. I expect not only a full refund but compensation for the distress and inconvenience and out of pocket expense.

I look forward to hearing from you within the next fourteen days failing which I will refer this matter to ABTA and/or my solicitor.

Yours faithfully

Chapter 5 - Buying A Car

27 Dissatisfaction Villas
Gripe Street
Moan City
TX9 3XX

Dear Sir

Ford Fiesta - M726 XXX

You will recall that I purchased the above vehicle from you on April 1st in the sum of £6999. What an April fool it's turned out to be.

I have returned it to your workshop on no fewer than seven occasions in the last month - one of the tyres was bald, the steering rack had to be replaced, the windscreen had an illegal crack in it, the radio cassette player didn't work, the sunroof leaked and one of the panels is a different colour from the rest of the car. I have repeatedly tried to reject the vehicle and claim a refund but you have denied me my rights. If you fail to do so within the next fourteen days I will refer the matter to the Retail Motor Industry Federation for their opinion. I will also reserve my rights to sue claiming a full refund. Alternatively you could offer to put the car into A1 condition and compensate me for the time that the vehicle has been off the road and has been of less than satisfactory quality.

I look forward to hearing from you by return.

Yours faithfully

Chapter 6 - The Professionals

27 Dissatisfaction Villas
Gripe Street
Moan City
TX9 3XX

Dear Madam

22 Acacia Avenue

I instructed you to carry out the purchase of the above property about twelve weeks ago. You assured me that there would be no problem with the conveyancing and that I would be able to complete within four weeks of instructing you. I'm still waiting. The vendor is now on the verge of cancelling the deal because of the delay. I would be grateful if you could clarify in writing the following points;

1. *Why there have been so many delays with the conveyancing.*
2. *What remains to be done and what you propose to do to speed things up.*
3. *Can you confirm that I will not be charged any more than the agreed fee of £299.*
4. *I expect some form of compensation for the delay.*

I look forward to hearing from you by return.

Yours faithfully

Chapter 7 - Health

27 Dissatisfaction Villas
Gripe Street
Moan City
TX9 3XX

Dear Sir

SuperDuper Spectacles - £199

I'm writing to confirm my oral complaint at your premises of earlier today. In essence, the spectacles which you have supplied do not match my prescription. They give me a headache and make me feel nauseous. You stated that my eyes would simply take time to adjust to the new lenses but they are clearly unacceptable. If you are unprepared to put the correct prescription lenses into the frames I'll be forced to go to another optician to get him to do the job properly. The associated costs will be sought from you, if necessary through the courts.

I fully anticipate being able to resolve this matter on an amicable basis.

Yours faithfully

Chapter 8 - Finance And Insurance Services

27 Dissatisfaction Villas
Gripe Street
Moan City
TX9 3XX

Dear Sir/Madam

Account Number: 677782496

Please find enclosed copies of correspondence with my local branch where my account is held. You will note that for the past month there have been unauthorised withdrawals from my account using several ATM's. As I made clear to my branch manager, I was in Saudi Arabia at the time on business and the card never left my possession. I have not divulged my details to anybody. I therefore expect you to re-credit my account with these unauthorised withdrawals and give me an undertaking that I will not suffer any problems in the future. If I do not receive your satisfactory confirmation I will refer the matter to the Office of the Banking Ombudsman.

Yours faithfully

Glossary Of Terms

APR. Annual percentage rate (APR) allows consumers to compare the real cost of borrowing. The higher the APR quoted for a loan or a credit card, the more expensive the credit.

Arbitration. A means of settling disputes other than through the courts. Both parties have to agree to arbitration.

Betterment. Gaining from a defect in a consumer purchase. For example, putting a more powerful engine into a car whose original motor has failed.

Caveat Emptor. *"Let the buyer beware"*. Purchasers have to take care before signing on the dotted line.

Charge Card. Operates like a credit card in that a period of grace is allowed for repayment but the whole of the amount charged each month must be repaid. Examples are American Express and Diners Club.

Consideration. The amount paid under a contract to fulfil its obligations. For example cash is the usual form of consideration when buying goods and services.

Cooling-off Period. The time in which you are entitled to cancel certain finance agreements.

Credit Card. A means of paying for goods and services whereby the retailer's bill is paid by the credit card issuer. The user has a period of time to either settle the debt when it becomes due or to pay off a minimum amount with the balance accruing interest. Usually an annual fee is payable.

Debit Card. A card used for payment for goods and services in much the same way as a cheque. It is not governed by the Consumer Credit Act. Examples are Switch and Connect.

Defendant. The person against whom a civil action is brought.

Environmental Health Officer. Employed by local authorities to police environmental legislation such as noise and air pollution, food hygiene etc.

Estimate. An informal 'best guess' of the likely charge for a job. Cannot be relied upon.

Hire Purchase. A way of funding a consumer purchase. Importantly, it is the finance company which owns the goods until the last payment has been made.

Indemnity Basis. This is a type of insurance whereby a deduction is made for wear and tear. This differs from "new for old" policies.

Invitation to Treat. A price indicated on goods for sale is merely an "invitation to treat" from a proposed purchaser. It does not mean that the retailer is obliged to sell at that price and effectively it is like tendering for bids. The contract is formed once the consumer has made an offer which has been accepted by the retailer (this may be the precise amount of the invitation to treat or less or more).

Judgment. The formal award of the court.

Legal Tender. The offer of payment in a form which a retailer is obliged to accept. Bank of England notes and gold coins are legal tender for the payment of any amount whilst cupro-nickel and bronze coins are legal tender for relatively small amounts. The retailer is not *obliged* to give change - the exact sum must be tendered.

Letter Before Action. Sent to the person who owes you money or is required to do something as a final opportunity before court papers are issued.

Litigant In Person. A plaintiff who acts without the support of a solicitor whether paid or unpaid.

Mitigation of Loss. When a consumer suffers a loss as a result of somebody or something being in breach of contract, there is a common law duty to act to reduce that loss. For example if a house is flooded, checking into the nearest 5 star hotel and running up a huge bar bill is not good evidence of mitigation of loss.

Negligence. When reasonable skill and care is not taken (the standard varies according to the individual circumstances) and damage which is reasonably foreseeable results.

Plaintiff. The person bringing civil proceedings.

Quote. A fixed price for a specified job.

Right of Lien. The right of a repairer or professional to hold onto a consumer's goods until his fees have been settled.

Ringing. When stolen cars are given new identities from written-off or scrapped vehicles.

Satisfaction Note. Usually issued by builders on completion of work to indicate that the consumer accepts the work to his or her satisfaction.

Title. The legal term for ownership of goods and property.

Trading Standards Officer. Employed by local authorities to police consumer legislation. For example they will prosecute tour operators for publishing misleading information in holiday brochures.

Warranty. A guarantee or assurance that a certain term with reference to the goods supplied will be of a certain standard. A breach of warranty gives rise to a claim for damages i.e. financial compensation but not to a right to reject the goods and treat the contract as repudiated.

Without Prejudice. Used in negotiating a settlement to a dispute. Proposals made and not accepted cannot later be relied on in court that one party has admitted liability.

Further Reading

Legal books can be quite heavy going and written principally for lawyers rather than lay consumers. But there are plenty of good sources of reference available. In addition to the following, local libraries usually stock countless useful leaflets, factsheets and contact addresses. Newspapers and periodicals too, particularly if kept on CD-Rom, often provide a convenient way of keeping up to date on changes in the law and procedure. Local law centres, Citizens' Advice Bureaux, solicitors offering free legal surgeries and providers of telephone legal advice should all also be considered.

Lowe and Woodroffe, *Consumer Law & Practice*, (Sweet & Maxwell)

Oxford Dictionary of Law, (Oxford University Press)

Pritchard, *The Penguin Guide to the Law*, (Penguin)

Know Your Rights, (Reader's Digest)

Redmond, *General Principles of English Law*, (M and E Handbooks)

Richards, *350 Legal Problems Solved*, (Consumers' Association)